COMPACT *Research*

# Teen Violence

**Teenage Problems**

ReferencePoint
Press®

San Diego, CA

## Other books in the Compact Research Teenage Problems set:

Teenage Alcoholism
Teenage Dropouts
Teenage Drug Abuse
Teenage Eating Disorders
Teenage Mental Illness
Teenage Sex and Pregnancy
Teenage Suicide

*For a complete list of titles please visit www.referencepointpress.com.

COMPACT *Research*

# Teen Violence

## Carla Mooney

### Teenage Problems

ReferencePoint Press®

San Diego, CA

**For more information, contact:**
ReferencePoint Press, Inc.
PO Box 27779
San Diego, CA 92198
www.ReferencePointPress.com

LIBRARY OF CONGRESS CATALOGING-IN-PUBLICATION DATA

Mooney, Carla, 1970–
   Teen violence : by Carla Mooney.
     pages cm. -- (Compact research) (What is teenage violence? -- How serious is teenage violence? -- How does media influence teenage violence? -- Can teenage violence be stopped?)
   Includes bibliographical references and index.
   ISBN 978-1-60152-496-6 (hbk.) -- ISBN 1-60152-496-X (hbk.)
 1. Juvenile delinquency--Juvenile literature. 2. Violence--Juvenile literature. I. Title.
  HV9069.M66  2013
  364.36--dc23

                                     2012033700

# Contents

# Foreword

"**Where is the knowledge we have lost in information?**"

—T.S. Eliot, "The Rock."

As modern civilization continues to evolve, its ability to create, store, distribute, and access information expands exponentially. The explosion of information from all media continues to increase at a phenomenal rate. By 2020 some experts predict the worldwide information base will double every seventy-three days. While access to diverse sources of information and perspectives is paramount to any democratic society, information alone cannot help people gain knowledge and understanding. Information must be organized and presented clearly and succinctly in order to be understood. The challenge in the digital age becomes not the creation of information, but how best to sort, organize, enhance, and present information.

ReferencePoint Press developed the *Compact Research* series with this challenge of the information age in mind. More than any other subject area today, researching current issues can yield vast, diverse, and unqualified information that can be intimidating and overwhelming for even the most advanced and motivated researcher. The *Compact Research* series offers a compact, relevant, intelligent, and conveniently organized collection of information covering a variety of current topics ranging from illegal immigration and deforestation to diseases such as anorexia and meningitis.

The series focuses on three types of information: objective single-author narratives, opinion-based primary source quotations, and facts and statistics. The clearly written objective narratives provide context and reliable background information. Primary source quotes are carefully selected and cited, exposing the reader to differing points of view, and facts and statistics sections aid the reader in evaluating perspectives. Presenting these key types of information creates a richer, more balanced learning experience.

For better understanding and convenience, the series enhances information by organizing it into narrower topics and adding design features that make it easy for a reader to identify desired content. For example, in *Compact Research: Illegal Immigration*, a chapter covering the economic impact of illegal immigration has an objective narrative explaining the various ways the economy is impacted, a balanced section of numerous primary source quotes on the topic, followed by facts and full-color illustrations to encourage evaluation of contrasting perspectives.

The ancient Roman philosopher Lucius Annaeus Seneca wrote, "It is quality rather than quantity that matters." More than just a collection of content, the *Compact Research* series is simply committed to creating, finding, organizing, and presenting the most relevant and appropriate amount of information on a current topic in a user-friendly style that invites, intrigues, and fosters understanding.

# Teen Violence at a Glance

## Teen Violence Defined

Violent behavior in teens can include a wide range of behaviors, including temper tantrums, physical aggression, fighting, threats, attempts to hurt others, use of weapons, cruelty toward animals, and destruction of property.

## Seriousness

According to the Centers for Disease Control and Prevention (CDC), youth violence is a leading cause of injury, disability, and premature death among young people in the United States.

## Causes

Most experts believe that teen violence is caused by a combination of individual, family, and community factors.

## Choosing Violence

Violence is a choice. Teens choose violence to release pent-up anger and frustration, control another person, or retaliate for a perceived injury or slight.

## Gangs

Gangs are responsible for the majority of serious teen violence in the United States. Gang activity includes robbery, drugs and gun trafficking, fraud, extortion, and prostitution.

## Dating Violence

Dating violence is a widespread problem among teens. It occurs when one person uses a pattern of destructive behaviors to exert power and control over a romantic partner.

## Violent Media and Teens

Numerous studies have concluded that violent images in the media lead to an increase in aggressive and violent behavior in teens, but critics say the link has not been scientifically proved.

## Electronic Aggression

Widespread use of social media, cell phones, and e-mail has led to a new form of violence—electronic aggression. Electronic aggression is any type of harassment or bullying that occurs through electronic sources.

## Prevention

Effective ways to prevent teen violence include teaching teens interpersonal and conflict resolution skills, developing positive role models in teens' lives, and empowering and educating communities about teen violence.

# Overview

Friends say that eighteen-year-old Bobby Tillman usually went out of his way to avoid violence. Yet in November 2010 Tillman walked into a fight he did not see coming. Tillman was walking past a house party in Douglass County, Georgia, when a fight broke out between two female partygoers. When one of the girls struck a male partygoer, the young man refused to hit her back but announced he would strike the next male that he saw. That unsuspecting victim was Tillman. Witnesses say Tillman did not see the punch coming. He struggled to keep his balance but was quickly pushed to the ground. Three more teens jumped into the fight. They kicked, punched, and stomped Tillman so badly that one of his bones broke and pierced his heart. He died later that night.

The violence that ended Tillman's life also destroyed the lives of his teenage attackers. Police arrested the four attackers, and they now face life in prison if convicted. As of September 2012 two have been sentenced to life in prison. The violence that killed Tillman was senseless, says Douglass County district attorney David McDade. "Young people that had a life ahead of them, on both sides," McDade said. "This is an absolutely unprovoked, senseless killing by young people killing another young man for no reason, no motive."[1]

## What Is Teen Violence?

Teen violence seems to be a constant feature in the news. Reports of school shootings, gang activity, and street violence appear in headlines around the country. On a daily basis, teen violence might seem more prevalent in inner cities but in reality it affects urban and suburban communities, low-income and wealthier people, and people of various racial and ethnic backgrounds. "Youth violence . . . is something that affects communities big and small, and people of all races and all colors. It is an American problem,"[2] says US attorney general Eric Holder.

Teenage violence can take many forms. Some teens explode in violent temper tantrums when angry. Violent teens may become physically aggressive, threatening others with bodily harm. Some follow through on their threats and attempt to hurt others in a fight, throwing punches, kicking, and stomping to inflict injury. Adding weapons such as knives and guns to a fight vastly increases the chances of serious injury and death.

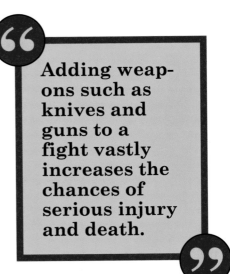

> **Adding weapons such as knives and guns to a fight vastly increases the chances of serious injury and death.**

Other times teen violence is directed at animals, property, or objects. Violent teens often start by abusing animals before escalating to crimes against people. Other teens engage in destructive behavior such as arson and vandalism.

Crimes such as robbery and assault are other examples of teen violence. Still another is bullying, which might not result in physical injury to the victim but can cause serious, long-lasting emotional damage.

*Teen violence takes many forms but often involves physical aggression toward another person and the use of deadly weapons. As a leading cause of injury, disability, and premature death among young people in the United States, teen violence is of serious concern.*

## How Serious Is Teen Violence?

Youth violence has a significant impact on teens, their families and friends, communities, and society in general. According to the Centers for Disease Control and Prevention (CDC), youth violence is a leading cause of injury, disability, and premature death among young people in the United States. According to a 2010 fact sheet from the CDC, over a one-year period more than 658,000 teens were treated in emergency rooms for injuries related to violence.

The effects of teen violence can be severe and lasting. Many teens die from violence. In the United States, homicide is the second leading cause of death behind accidents for youth aged ten to twenty-four. Violence also injures many teens and innocent bystanders. Some of these injuries leave the victim with long-term disabilities. Teen violence can also cause emotional, social, and behavioral problems in youth. These problems can increase the chance that a teen will engage in violent acts in the future. In addition, youth involved in violence, both as victims and perpetrators, have a higher risk of developing mental health problems such as depression and anxiety. They are also more likely to abuse drugs and alcohol.

## Culture of Violence

Violence has always been part of American culture. Action movies such as *Terminator* and *Transformers* splash violence across movie screens. War games and toy guns encourage violent play. Even one of America's most popular sports, football, features violent hits between players that draw cheers from fans. "Listen, people love the violence," says R. Todd Jewell, a sports economist at the University of North Texas in Denton. "Football is the most popular sport in the United States, and it's popular because of the violence."[3]

These activities are often described as part of a culture of violence that is unique to the United States. In the opinion of some, this culture has led to American society becoming desensitized to violence and more likely to resort to it. "The misuse of power through violent action is taught through and supported by culture. The United States is one of the most violent cultures in the Western world with more crimes being committed with guns and through violent force,"[4] says psychologist Ofer Zur. No other developed country experiences as much violence as the United States—especially gun violence. A study in the *Journal of Trauma and Acute Care Surgery*, for instance, found that the gun murder rate in the United States is about twenty times higher than the next twenty-two richest and most populated countries combined.

> " Teen violence can also cause emotional, social, and behavioral problems in youth. "

## What Causes Teen Violence?

Although no one factor can predict teen violence, several risk factors make a teen more likely to engage in violent behavior. One of the biggest predictors of teen violence is prior violent behavior. Teens who have shown a tendency to solve problems through violence or to exhibit aggressive behavior in the past are more likely to react violently in the future. According to the Kansas Safe School Resource Center, an organization that promotes safe and nonviolent schools, "Unless provided with support and counseling, a youth who has a history of aggressive and violent behavior is likely to repeat those behaviors."[5]

> **Experts caution that having one or more risk factors for violence does not mean that a teen will actually become violent.**

In the same way, teens who find themselves surrounded by violence, whether in the home, neighborhood, or school, are more likely to see violence as an acceptable behavior. Often these teens do not learn to resolve conflicts peacefully and instead resort to violence to settle disputes. "When children see someone resolve conflict with aggression, they are more likely to learn that behavior," says Joan Durrant, clinical child psychologist. "So the more a child sees someone resolving conflict with aggression, the more aggressive they become."[6] Other risk factors center on the friends and the choices a teen makes. Teens who hang out with juvenile delinquents or join gangs are more likely to engage in violent behavior. Often violent acts are required for membership in gangs, where violence will bring a teen prestige and respect. In addition, using drugs and alcohol can increase a teen's aggressive and violent tendencies. Alcohol and drugs lower a person's inhibitions, making him or her more likely to strike out or act with less self-control.

Experts caution that having one or more risk factors for violence does not mean that a teen will actually become violent. Instead, experts say, teens with a higher risk of violence may need intervention and counseling to teach them skills to solve problems and resolve conflict peacefully.

## Choosing Violence

Violence is a choice that teens make. Instead of calling the police, involving a parent, teacher, or other adult, or approaching a problem in a peaceful way, some teens choose violent behavior to resolve conflicts.

Teens may choose violent and aggressive behavior for different reasons. Some teens use violence as a way to release pent-up feelings of anger or frustration. Teens with poor social and academic skills may be frustrated at school. Any little slight by a classmate may cause such a teen to erupt violently, possibly starting a fight to express his or her pent-up emotions.

Other times, teens use violence as a way to control someone or get something that they want. In cases of dating violence, an aggressive boyfriend may use violence or the threat of violence to manipulate his girlfriend—to control what she does, to whom she talks, how she dresses, and where she goes.

One of the most common reasons teens choose violence is to retaliate for a real or perceived slight against them or someone they care about. For teens involved in gangs, an attack against a gang member can trigger even more violent acts of retaliation. A report released by the CDC in January 2012 concludes that the majority of gang homicides are the result of members retaliating against rival gangs. "Overall, these findings support a view of gang homicides as retaliatory violence. These incidents most often result when contentious gang members pass each other in public places and a conflict quickly escalates into homicide with the use of firearms and drive-by shootings,"[7] write the report's authors.

## How Do Media Influence Teen Violence?

Today's teens live in a world saturated with multiple media including music, video games, television, movies, and the Internet. Over the years, violence in the media has become more common. Today's television programming aimed at youth, from cartoons to Nickelodeon's live-action shows, contains many violent images, such as fighting and blowing up objects. Prime-time crime investigation shows and hospital dramas feature fights, weapons, and murders. In addition, technology such as on-demand programming and DVRs allow youth to access many violent programs intended for adults. As a result, the American Academy of Pediatrics reports the average American child will have viewed about two hundred thousand acts of violence on television by age eighteen.

Parents and child development experts are worried about the effect of so much media violence on today's youth. Numerous studies have reported that viewing violence in the media leads to an increase in aggressive

*Some experts contend that violent video games lead to violent or aggressive youth behavior, while others argue that only seriously troubled teens might be influenced by such games. Studies on this topic are ongoing.*

attitudes, values, and behavior, especially in youth. Moreover, some researchers have concluded that viewing violence in the media also has long-lasting effects on behavior and personality. They believe that these effects occur because viewing violence repeatedly desensitizes the viewer to it. This may lead to teens not taking violence seriously and being less likely to intervene on behalf of a victim. Viewing violence may also increase a viewer's tendency to become violent or to expose him- or herself to violent activities.

> " **Teens who bully have an increased risk of substance abuse, poor grades, and being involved in future violence as teens and adults.** "

At the same time, critics argue that a link between violence in the media and teen violence has not been proved. They point out that serious violent crimes among youth decreased between 1996 and 2012, while at the same time television programming and video game sales skyrocketed. "Looking at the data as a criminologist, I have to say that the evidence does not demonstrate a measurable effect of any type of violent media on *violent crime*,"[8] says American University criminologist Joanne Savage.

## Bullies and Violence

Bullying, a form of aggression and violence that affects teens across America, is defined as an ongoing pattern of harassment and abuse. Bullies can attack their victims directly through physical or verbal attacks. They may also attack victims indirectly, by spreading rumors or posting harassing or humiliating information online. According to a 2012 report from the National Center for Education Statistics, approximately 23 percent of public schools reported that bullying occurred among students on a daily or weekly basis.

Bullying can result in physical injury, emotional distress, and social anxiety. Teens who are victims of bullying are more likely to develop mental health disorders such as depression and anxiety or to complain of psychosomatic illnesses such as headaches. They are more likely to have difficulty adjusting to the school environment. Bullying also affects the aggressors. Teens who bully have an increased risk of substance abuse, poor grades, and being involved in future violence as teens and adults.

In some cases bullying can even lead to death. While there are no specific statistics on suicide and bullying, the CDC reports that suicide is the third leading cause of death among people between the ages of ten and twenty-four, with males consti-

> "Electronic aggression is defined as any type of harassment or bullying that occurs through e-mail, chat rooms, instant messaging, websites, blogs, or text messages."

tuting approximately 84 percent of the deaths. According to Melissa Reeves, a school psychologist and expert on bullying, bullying can be a significant factor in youth suicide when teens feel they cannot escape from it. "When they really get to a sense of hopelessness and helplessness, you know, where they see no other way out of this particular situation, then, unfortunately that is when we do see completed suicides,"[9] says Reeves.

In 2012 Texas high school freshman Teddy Molina shot and killed himself with a hunting rifle. His family says that for years he had been hounded by school bullies who made fun of him for his Korean-Hispanic heritage and threatened to hurt or kill him. Molina's sister, Misa, says that the bullying had intensified so much in recent months that Molina had said several times that he wanted to kill himself because of it. Since his death, Molina's family has organized antibullying rallies. "We don't need any more people dying because kids can't stop being mean to each other," says Misa, "Hopefully, this will teach them a lesson that a life is very precious and we should hold onto that, we should keep that in our hearts to make . . . each and every one of us a better person."[10]

## Electronic Violence

Today, teens use cell phones and the Internet to communicate instantly with people across the country and around the world. Text messaging, chat rooms, and social networking allow teens to connect with family and friends from anyplace, anytime. This technology can help teens develop and maintain friendships. Internet access allows teens to do research quickly and to learn about a wide variety of subjects.

At the same time, the widespread adoption of cell phones and the Internet has led to a new arena for youth violence—electronic violence. Electronic aggression is defined as any type of harassment or bullying that occurs through e-mail, chat rooms, instant messaging, websites, blogs, or text messages. Using electronic media, youth can embarrass, harass, or threaten their peers. Teens can post humiliating pictures on social networking sites for all to see. They can send harassing or threatening text messages. They can forward private messages with embarrassing pictures or information to other teens.

An increasing number of teens are being affected by electronic violence and bullying. In a study of electronic aggression, the CDC reports that up to 35 percent of young people say they have been victims of electronic aggression. Like other forms of youth violence, electronic violence can result in emotional distress and behavior problems at school. Students who have

> " Community mentoring programs match teens and adults who can demonstrate positive behavior. "

been harassed through electronic media are more likely to get detention or suspension, skip school, and experience emotional distress than teens who have not. "It is clear that youth are underestimating the level of harm associated with cyberbullying," says Jennifer Shapka, an associate professor in the Department of Education at the University of British Columbia. "Students need to be educated that this 'just joking' behavior has serious implications,"[11] she adds.

Electronic aggression also may lead to physical bullying. The CDC reports that perpetrators of electronic aggression are more likely to engage in face-to-face aggression.

## Posting Fights Online

With the soaring popularity of YouTube, anyone with a cell phone can film a quick video and post it on the Internet for the world to see. Nationwide, many teens have used cell phones and video cameras to post videos of violent fights online. "They see friends getting a lot of attention from the posting of these violent attacks, and being young and impressionable kids, they figure that's one way of getting attention themselves,"[12] says

Gerry Leone, the district attorney of Middlesex, Massachusetts.

In January 2012 six teens beat and robbed another teen in an alley behind a Chicago elementary school. The beating and robbery were bad enough. But then a seventh teen videotaped the attack, which was posted online. The video showed the victim being punched, kicked, and dragged down the alley. "There is shock value for those of us as adults, going, 'Wow.' But kids think there's something kind of cool about it," says psychologist Jennifer Hartstein. "And now the Internet can bring them notoriety or some sort of fame, so it's making it harder to say, 'This is a bad thing.'"[13]

Police officers say that when teens post videos of themselves they are often looking for bragging rights and do not fully understand the consequences of their actions. "Everybody sees it. That's the evidence," says Alan Krok, a veteran Chicago police detective. "When it hits YouTube, (the youths involved in the crimes) don't think the whole thing through."[14]

## Can Teen Violence Be Stopped?

There is no one cause of teen violence, and as a result, efforts at prevention are just as varied. Training and counseling on social skills can teach teens how to handle tough social situations and to resolve conflicts in nonviolent ways. Parent and family-based counseling programs can improve family relationships, helping parents to model positive behavior and improve communication. Community mentoring programs match teens and adults who can demonstrate positive behavior.

Creating safe places for youth to gather, such as for after-school activities or at youth centers, can also reduce teen violence. In one Chicago neighborhood filled with gang violence, resident Diane Latiker started a program called Kids Off The Block. She opened her home to teens, giving them an unofficial after-school community center. On any given day, dozens of young people show up at her center. They work with tutors, practice job interviews, and take field trips to museums or movies. "It doesn't matter where they come from, what they've done. We've had six gangs in my living room at one time. . . . But that was the safe place. And you know what? They respected that,"[15] says Latiker.

# What Is Teen Violence?

On September 24, 2009, sixteen-year-old honors student Derrion Albert walked from school toward a local community center. He never made it. A cell phone video shows that as he neared the center, Albert was caught between two rival groups of teenagers. Dozens of angry teens had converged in a vacant lot in Chicago, Illinois. They pummeled each other with fists, feet, and two-by-four planks.

Eyewitnesses said that Albert was an innocent bystander, a teen who happened to be in the wrong place at the wrong time. One of the fighters struck Albert from behind with a board, knocking him unconscious. When Albert regained consciousness, he tried to stand but was attacked again by five teens. They again struck him in the head with a board, kicked him, and stomped on his head. By the time a witness dragged Albert to safety, it was too late. He died a short time later. "This gang violence is escalating beyond control," says T'Awannda Piper, the worker who pulled Albert into a building. "He was caught in it. The kids directly involved walked away healthy, and this kid didn't walk away at all."[16]

## Widespread Violence

Teen violence is a widespread problem in the United States. A 2010 study conducted by the Substance Abuse and Mental Health Services Administration (SAMHSA) found that nearly 7.8 million teens aged twelve to seventeen participated in at least one of three violent behaviors in a twelve-month period before the survey. Twenty percent reported being in a serious fight, 16 percent were involved in gang fights, and 7.5 percent said they had attacked another person with the intent to cause serious harm.

In June 2012 Dave Reynolds experienced firsthand the effects of teen violence. Reynolds was attacked by a group of twenty teens in Spokane, Washington. He had just finished his shift as a bouncer at a local club and was walking to his motorcycle when a group of teens approached him. One teen asked if he could have Reynolds's helmet. When Reynolds said no, another teen punched him in the head. "I was completely unconscious in the middle of the road and they were stomping me in the face and kicking me in the head," Reynolds says. When Reynolds' girlfriend tried to intervene, the teens knocked her unconscious as well. The violent attack left Reynolds with broken bones in his cheek, and nose, and around the eye socket. "It's a group of teenagers and . . . it doesn't seem it would be that big of a deal, but when they get into a large group or in a pack well . . . a lot of fists can do a lot of damage,"[17] says Reynolds.

> **Teen violence is a widespread problem in the United States.**

## Public Health Problem

Fifteen-year-old Yaviel Ivey lives in Chicago's Englewood neighborhood, in which violence is a daily occurrence. In one example, Yaviel says, "I saw this guy getting chased down the street by another dude who was firing a gun at him, and my mom was like 'What are you doing? Get down!' And, I got down."[18]

Teen violence is a serious public health problem. According to the CDC, homicide is the second leading cause of death for young people between the ages of ten and twenty-four. In a sixteen-month period, at least 80 people in Yaviel's neighborhood have been killed and 260 others have been wounded by gunfire, including 100 teenagers. "In the area I live in, I don't expect to have a future here, and I want better for myself,"[19] says Yaviel.

Violence that does not result in teen deaths frequently results in injuries. Injuries can include cuts, bruises, broken bones, and gunshot wounds. According to a 2010 CDC report, more than 656,000 young people aged ten to twenty-four were treated in emergency rooms for injuries sustained from violence in 2008.

Serious injuries such as gunshot wounds can cause lasting disabilities. Victims spend the rest of their lives struggling with physical, men-

> " **Serious injuries such as gunshot wounds can cause lasting disabilities.** "

tal, and emotional damage. They may be affected financially, if left with significant medical costs. In 2009 fourteen-year-old Ondelee Perteet of Chicago was shot in the face at a birthday party. The bullet severed his spine and left him paralyzed from the neck down. Three years later, Ondelee is still confined to a wheelchair and dependent on his mother for care. "There are so many things he can't do. He's the man of the house, but he can't help me with the groceries. He can't take the trash out. He can't play basketball. He can't go swimming. He got a life sentence in a chair,"[20] says his mother.

## Violence at School

On February 27, 2012, seventeen-year-old T.J. Lane walked up to a cafeteria table at Chardon High School in Ohio, pulled out a gun, and started shooting. "He was silent the entire time," says Nate Mueller, who was just a few feet away from Lane when the shooting started. "There was no warning or anything. He just opened fire."[21] Lane's shooting spree killed three students and injured several others.

Although school shootings like the one at Chardon High School grab national headlines, they are rare. According to the CDC, less than 1 percent of homicides and suicides of youth aged five to eighteen occur at school. Instead, the majority of school violence revolves around fights between students. In a nationwide CDC survey, 11 percent of teens in grades nine to twelve reported being in a physical fight on school property over the previous twelve months. When the fights include weapons, they have increased potential to cause significant injury or become deadly.

The threat of violence has made many teens afraid at school. In the same survey, the CDC found that 5 percent of teens did not go to school for one or more days during a one-month period because they felt unsafe. "It's ridiculous that you can't feel safe while your child is in school. That's ridiculous. It's unnecessary violence. It's a shame. It's sad,"[22] says Furman Pace, father of a Philadelphia middle school student.

School violence also affects teachers. According to the American Psychological Association, more than 25 percent of teachers are threatened on the job by students. Seven percent of teachers actually become victims of physical violence. In February 2012 a Philadelphia middle school teacher was punched repeatedly after a verbal argument with a fourteen-year-old student.

> According to research by the American Psychological Association, more than 25 percent of teachers are threatened on the job by students.

## Dating and Violence

Dating violence is a pattern of destructive behaviors used to exert power and control over a romantic partner. Dating violence can be physical, sexual, or psychological. Examples of dating violence include hitting or punching, forced sexual contact, bullying, or name-calling. It can take place in person or electronically, through e-mail or social media. "Everybody knows that if they see a bruise they're going to ask about a bruise," says Sherry Boston, solicitor general of DeKalb County, Georgia. "But there are also things which may not be physical." Other signs of dating violence include "stalking, or boyfriends or girlfriends that have a tight leash on each other by wanting to always know where they are, tracking them with the cell phone GPS, wanting to have passwords to access their emails or phone, sending threatening texts [and] Facebook issues,"[23] says Boston.

Dating violence is widespread among teens. According to a 2012 CDC publication, approximately 10 percent of adolescents reported being physically hurt by a boyfriend or girlfriend in a twelve-month period. Psychological abuse is even more common. According to a 2012 study of seventh graders, 37 percent reported being a victim of psychological dating violence. "It's an unspoken epidemic, and it's going on right in front of our faces,"[24] says Maritza Rivera, president of Aneesa Michelle's Group, a nonprofit organization that raises the public's awareness of teen dating violence.

The aggressor in a violent relationship can be either the girl or the boy. Some studies have found that girls commit violence against their partners slightly more frequently. Girls are more likely to hit, slap, kick, or yell at partners. Boys' violent acts, however, are more likely to involve beating up, choking or strangling, or sexually abusing a romantic partner.

An abusive or violent romantic relationship can have serious short-term and long-term effects on a teenager. Victims of dating violence are more likely to struggle in school, binge drink, engage in physical fighting, and attempt suicide. Victims may also carry the abuse and violence into future relationships.

## Violence Not Taken Seriously

Even if people are aware of dating violence, many do not take it seriously. Some dismiss the behavior as immaturity. Others blame the victim. For example, when pop star Rihanna was beaten by her boyfriend, singer Chris Brown, a poll of two hundred Boston teens found that almost half believed the assault was Rihanna's fault. Rivera says that many teens share that attitude. "They'll say, 'Why did she keep arguing with him if she knew he was violent?,'" Rivera says. "They say, 'She must have done something to make him so angry.'"[25]

When a boyfriend texts a girl repeatedly to check up on her whereabouts, parents and teens may dismiss the jealous behavior as puppy love. Inexperienced teens sometimes see controlling behavior as a sign of love. "Teens don't always have a strong sense of self, and they sometimes don't know what a healthy relationship is. Or, they would rather have an unpleasant relationship than not have one at all,"[26] says Elizabeth Richeson, a psychologist who became involved with dating-violence education after her granddaughter was murdered by an ex-boyfriend in 2006.

## Gang Violence

Gangs are responsible for the majority of serious teen violence in the United States. Gangs exist in every state. According to the FBI, the United States is home to about thirty-three thousand violent gangs with about 1.4 million members. Many are well organized and use violence to control neighborhoods and make money illegally. Gang activity includes robbery, drug and gun trafficking, fraud, extortion, and prostitution. According to the National Youth Gang Survey, two out of five gang members are under eighteen years old.

> **Teen violence ... reduces worker productivity, decreases property values, and disrupts social services.**

Gang violence can be deadly. As members, teens are expected to commit violent acts such as fighting or armed robbery. Gang fights can quickly escalate as members wield guns and knives. In Newburgh, New York, in January 2012, adolescent taunting between suspected gang members quickly escalated into a brawl. By the time the fight was over, seventeen-year-old Levi King Flores was dead from a stab wound. A thirteen-year-old was arrested and charged with his murder. For Newburgh, a city of approximately twenty-nine thousand residents, the violence was not unusual. According to local law enforcement, gang violence was responsible for most of the city's sixteen homicides in the past two years. The police also estimate that local gang members affiliated with national gangs outnumber city police by three to one. This number does not count the hundreds of Newburgh teens involved in locally formed gangs. According to Senator Charles Schumer, the situation in Newburgh is shocking. "There are reports of shootouts in the town streets, strings of robberies and gang assaults with machetes,"[27] Schumer says.

## Damage to Communities

In addition to causing injury and death, teen violence affects the communities where it occurs. Violence increases a community's health care costs, as victims require care from local emergency rooms and doctors. Teen violence also reduces worker productivity, decreases property values, and disrupts social services. Families are moving out of areas with high concentrations of teen violence. New families are reluctant to move into a high-crime neighborhood. Property values decrease for everyone in the community. As people move out of the community and violence on the streets disrupts activity, local businesses suffer from lower worker productivity and reduced sales. They may close or choose to move out of the area, leaving vacancies that are difficult to fill because new businesses are less likely to open in high-crime areas.

In 2012 a group of teens roamed downtown Spokane, Washington. Residents reported cars being broken into, knives being pulled on business patrons, and employees getting beat up. Business owners were concerned that violence would keep people away, reducing sales and damaging their livelihoods. "People [don't] want to get harassed when they go downtown, they don't want to worry about 'is someone going to try and steal something from me' or 'am I going to get a knife pulled on me?,'"[28] says Reynolds, the Spokane bouncer who was attacked by a group of teens in 2012.

## A Community Problem

Teen violence is a serious problem that affects people across the United States. Every member of a community is affected when teens spin out of control. "Youth violence is a national concern,"[29] says Matthew Stagner, executive director of Chapin Hall, an independent policy research center.

# What Is Teen Violence

**❝Even teens from high-income, suburban and rural fam-ilies are exposed to surprising amounts of violence.❞**

Jess Holland, "Stopping Teen Dating Violence," *Door County Daily News*, June 4, 2012. www.doorcountydailynews.com.

Holland is a youth advocate with HELP of Door County, Wisconsin, a domestic violence advocacy group.

**❝We are losing too many children to gun and gang re-lated violence. The life of any young person is not ex-pendable. We have to act and we have to act together.❞**

—Deval L. Patrick, "Youth Violence Prevention Announcement," May 9, 2011. www.mass.gov.

Patrick is governor of Massachusetts.

* Editor's Note: While the definition of a primary source can be narrowly or broadly defined, for the purposes of Compact Research, a primary source consists of: 1) results of original research presented by an organization or researcher; 2) eyewitness accounts of events, personal experience, or work experience; 3) first-person editorials offering pundits' opinions; 4) government officials presenting political plans and/or policies; 5) representatives of organizations presenting testimony or policy.

**❝In that casket, I'm looking at 13, 14, 15, 18, 19-year-old men and women dying on the streets of Chicago. That's what's so profound to me about the violence.❞**

—Ameena Matthews, interview by Terry Gross, "'The Interrupters': Keeping Peace on the Streets," NPR, February 10, 2012. www.npr.org.

Matthews is a member of Chicago's Ceasefire interrupters team and a former youth gang member.

**❝Youth violence has long lasting, devastating consequences—the alarming rates of violence found by this study reinforce the importance of our efforts to prevent violence.❞**

—Pamela S. Hyde in SAMHSA, "New National Study Reveals That Nearly One in Three Adolescents Participated in a Violent Behavior over the Past Year," SAMHSA press release, September 22, 2012. www.samhsa.gov.

Hyde is an administrator with the Substance Abuse and Mental Health Services Admistration (SAMHSA).

**❝School violence is today at a record low.❞**

—Heather Ann Thompson, "Criminalizing Kids: The Overlooked Reason for Failing Schools," *Dissent*, Fall 2011, p. 27.

Thompson is an associate professor of history in the Department of African American Studies and the Department of History at Temple University.

**❝Teens involved in violence are getting younger and younger, and it has come to the point where older residents are concerned in all communities.❞**

—Neal Hicks, "Youth on Violence: Few Recreational Options in Some Parts of Town," *Lexington Herald-Leader*, August 12, 2012. www.kentucky.com.

Hicks is a nineteen-year-old resident of Lexington, Kentucky, where youth violence is an increasing problem.

> 66 **Too many young people's lives are being ruined and even lost because of violence in this community.** 99

—Taylor Robinson, "Youth on Violence: Uphold Curfew for Younger Teens," *Lexington Herald-Leader*, August 12, 2012. www.kentucky.com.

Robinson is an eighteen-year-old survivor of youth violence from Kentucky.

> 66 **Violence is a chronic health issue that can lead to asthma, obesity, or depression in youth who are involved in it. It's an economic issue, costing our economy over $14 billion in medical costs and lost productivity.** 99

—Kathleen Sebelius, speech, "National Forum on Youth Violence Prevention," HHS.gov, April 2, 2012. www.hhs.gov.

Sebelius is secretary of the US Department of Health and Human Services.

# What Is Teen Violence?

- According to Futures without Violence, a nonprofit group that works to end violence, approximately **one in three** adolescent girls in the United States is a victim of physical, emotional, or verbal abuse from a dating partner.

- Boys are more likely to inflict injuries because of **dating violence** than girls, reports Futures without Violence.

- Nearly **one in ten** high school students has been hit, slapped, or physically hurt on purpose by a boyfriend or girlfriend, according to Futures without Violence.

- According to the CDC, **homicide** is the second leading cause of death for young people aged ten to twenty-four.

- More than seven hundred thousand young people aged ten to twenty-four were treated in emergency departments in 2010 for injuries sustained due to violence, reports the CDC.

- An average of sixteen people aged ten to twenty-four are **murdered each day**, according to CDC reports.

- According to the US Department of Health and Human Services, **17.5 percent** of youth reported carrying a weapon on one or more days in a one-month period.

# Most Common Violent Crimes Among Youth

Young people between the ages of ten and seventeen are more likely to be arrested for aggravated assault than other violent crimes, according to statistics compiled by the Office of Juvenile Justice and Delinquency Prevention. Aggravated assault is an attack that results in serious physical harm and usually involves a weapon such as a gun or knife.

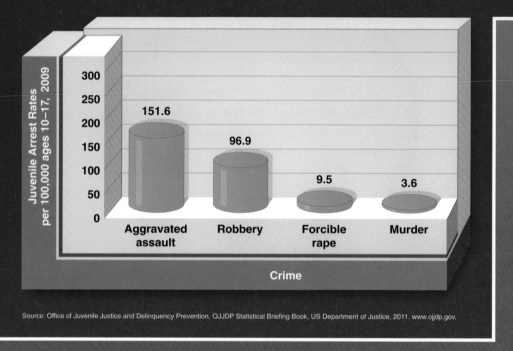

Source: Office of Juvenile Justice and Delinquency Prevention, OJJDP Statistical Briefing Book, US Department of Justice, 2011. www.ojjdp.gov.

- An estimated **20 percent** of high school students reported being bullied on school property, according to a CDC survey.

- The CDC reports that most **school-associated homicides** are caused by gunshot wounds, stabbing or cutting, and beating.

- The National Gang Center estimates that about **32 percent** of all cities, suburban areas, towns, and rural counties experience gang problems.

# Gang Problems in America

A concern for many communities is the presence of gangs. Despite prevention efforts, gang activity and violence remain high in many communities. A 2010 survey by the National Gang Center found that 34.1 percent of cities reported gang activity. Larger cities reported greater rates of gang activity and serious gang crimes. The study also found that after some initial decline in the late 1990s, gang activity remained relatively constant from 2005 through 2010.

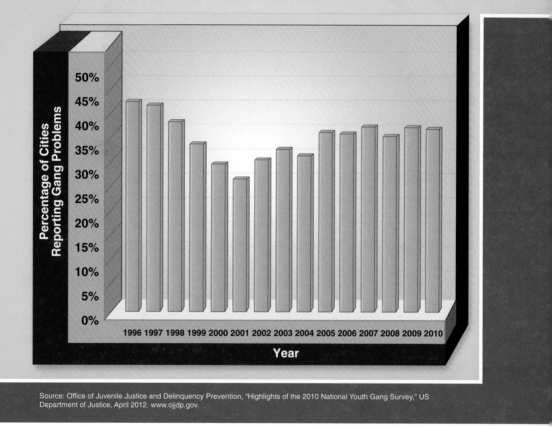

Source: Office of Juvenile Justice and Delinquency Prevention, "Highlights of the 2010 National Youth Gang Survey," US Department of Justice, April 2012. www.ojjdp.gov.

- According to the Child Trends Data Bank, about **33 percent** of high school students reported being in a physical fight over a one-year period.

- Teens can **purchase a handgun** on the streets for as little as fifty dollars, says Seattle gang expert Gabe Morales.

# What Causes Teen Violence?

> **"I think he just had an anger problem and was looking for revenge. He tried to shoot everyone that was on the porch that night when his friend got shot."**
>
> —Corshana Hatter, seventeen-year-old survivor of a drive-by shooting.

> **"Adolescents in controlling or violent relationships may carry these dangerous and unhealthy patterns into future relationships."**
>
> —Barack Obama, forty-fourth president of the United States.

Determining the causes behind teen violence is not a simple task. Most experts believe that several factors interact to determine a teen's risk of violent behavior. According to the CDC, individual risk factors such as frustration from learning or attention-deficit disorders can lead to teen violence. In many cases, teens do not learn how to deal with these frustrations in healthy ways and instead act out in anger.

Environmental factors may also increase a teen's risk for violence. Being surrounded by violence in the family, school, or community increases the likelihood a teen will become violent. Other environmental factors include a teen's peer group, access to firearms, and socioeconomic status.

A study by Duke University in Durham, North Carolina, supports the belief that no single factor explains why some children grow up to be violent teenagers. Instead, researchers found that a complex combination of factors increases a child's risk. In the study, researchers followed a group of 750 children from pre-school through high school. "None of these children is highly violent as a four-year-old," says Kenneth Dodge, director of the Center for Child and Family Policy at Duke University and the study's lead author. "The question is: how is it that some four-year-olds, who display only minor behavioral problems but are otherwise cute and cuddly, still grow into violent teenagers?" The researchers found that a complex interaction of factors led to a teen's violent behavior. "What we found is that small problems cumulate into more serious problems. There's not one single factor,"[30] Dodge says.

## Individual Risk Factors

Certain individual factors and characteristics may increase a teen's risk of becoming violent. Researchers say that one of the greatest predictors of future violent behavior is a previous history of violence, as an aggressor, victim, or bystander. Teens who come from violent families, who associate with violent peers, or who live in violent communities have a greater risk of becoming violent themselves.

Other individual factors that increase a teen's risk of violence include a number of cognitive and behavioral disorders, including attention-deficit disorder, hyperactivity, learning disorders, or other deficits in social, cognitive, or information-processing abilities. Experts believe that these disorders may impact a teen's impulse control, making him or her more likely to act out. They may also cause frustration, which can lead to aggression and violence. In addition, teens with emotional distress or a history of treatment for emotional problems are more likely to exhibit violent behavior.

> **Most experts believe that several factors interact to determine a teen's risk of violent behavior.**

## Drugs and Alcohol

Numerous studies have shown that when drugs and alcohol are involved, teen violence drastically increases. According to the National Survey on Drug Use and Health, youths aged twelve to seventeen who used an illegal drug were almost twice as likely to engage in violent behavior as compared with youth who did not use illegal drugs. In addition, the survey reported that the likelihood of engaging in violent behavior increased with the number of illegal drugs used.

Not every teen who uses alcohol or illegal drugs becomes violent. However, using these substances can increase a teen's risk of violent behavior because these substances lower inhibitions. In addition, violent behavior triggered by drugs and alcohol tends to be more severe and to last longer than violent behavior in which drugs and alcohol are not involved.

Using drugs and alcohol may also intensify other violence risk factors. Research has found that teens who are more likely to abuse these substances are also more likely to exhibit antisocial and risk-taking behaviors.

## Family Background

Family experiences contribute to how teens learn to think, feel, trust, and relate to others. Negative experiences over a sustained period of time may have a long-term psychological impact on them.

Many violent teens come from families where domestic abuse is present. Numerous studies suggest that children of violent parents have a higher risk of becoming violent. Experts believe this occurs because violence is a learned behavior. Children who watch family members behaving violently learn to model that behavior. They come to see violent behavior as acceptable. "Children with high-conflict parents are more likely to think that aggressive responses would be good ways to handle social conflicts,"[31] says John Bates, a professor of psychology at Indiana University's Department of Psychological and Brain Sciences.

> **Researchers say that one of the greatest predictors of future violent behavior is a previous history of violence, as an aggressor, victim, or bystander.**

The parent-child relationship can also affect whether a teen becomes violent. Children whose parents are distant or lax may not learn impulse control and feel that they can behave in any manner they want. Children subjected to harsh punishment may learn to see aggressive behavior as acceptable. According to a study published in the *Canadian Medical*

*Association Journal* in 2012, using corporal punishment can increase aggression in children. "We find children who are physically punished get more aggressive over time and those who are not physically punished get less aggressive over time,"[32] says Joan Durrant, the study's lead author.

## Peer and Social Risk Factors

By the time children reach adolescence, peers have a strong influence over them. Teens want to fit in, model peers they admire, or have what others have. The pressure to conform can be a powerful influence over a teen's behavior. Sometimes, the pressure to conform can lead to violence.

One of the differences between adult violence and teen violence is that teens are more likely to commit violent acts when with a group of their peers. Many teens will do something that is risky, violent, or illegal when with their friends that they would not do alone. This explains why a teen who hangs out with peers who view violence as acceptable has a higher risk of becoming violent. "Group pressure can override common sense fairly easily for these folks. . . . Teens tend not to have developed a clear sense of right and wrong,"[33] says Jay Reeve, a psychologist at Bradley Hospital at Brown University.

According to the US Surgeon General's office, teens who have weak social ties, who are not involved in many social activities, or who are unpopular at school are also more likely to become violent. These teens may find acceptance with antisocial or delinquent peer groups from whom they face peer pressure to commit violent acts.

## Involvement with Gangs

Becoming involved with a gang can greatly increase a teen's chances of participating in violent behavior. Gangs are responsible for the majority of the serious violence in the United States. According to the 2010 National Youth Gang Survey, there were more than twenty-nine thousand gangs with approximately 756,000 members across the United States. Research on gang activity has found that gang members are consistently more likely than other teens to engage in criminal activity and violence. "I was shot three times in 1997. I was shot once in 2002. I was shot 12 times in 2012. . . . To me it's just a steady flow of violence. I mean, I can't tell if it's worse or if it's not worse,"[34] says one current Chicago gang member.

Gang members are expected to be violent and fight rival gangs or rob stores at gunpoint. Frequent gang conflict leads to many preventable deaths. According to a 2012 CDC study, more than 90 percent of gang homicide victims were young males.

## Access to Firearms

When teens exhibit violent behavior, the presence of guns can intensify the violence. A fistfight may leave bruises or broken bones, but a gunfight can be lethal. According to a 2012 report by the Children's Defense Fund, 5,740 children and teens were killed in the United States by guns in 2008 and 2009. Two-thirds of them were victims of homicide. In addition, more than 34,000 children and teens were injured by guns in 2008 and 2009. These findings "speak to the importance of addressing youth if we really want to do something about the gun violence problem,"[35] says Linda L. Dahlberg, the associate director for science in CDC's Division of Violence Prevention.

Also, innocent bystanders are more likely to be injured or killed when guns are involved. "I was walking home, and all of a sudden shots were fired. My first natural reaction was to start running. As I began to run, I heard more shots, and then I felt a bullet rip through my leg. Once I made it to safety, I was simply happy to be alive. Here's what I don't get: I am not affiliated with gangs. I am a youth leader in my community, and enrolled in college. How could something like this happen to me? Are any of us safe?,"[36] asks nineteen-year-old Bryan James, a shooting survivor from Chicago, Illinois.

> **Becoming involved with a gang can greatly increase a teen's chances of participating in violent behavior.**

According to the Teen Gun Survey 2012 by UCAN, a Chicago-based social service organization, teens are finding it increasingly easy to obtain handguns. The percentage of teens who reported that they could get a gun increased from 34 percent to 44 percent. "People can get stolen guns for 50, 100 bucks," says Gabe Morales, a local gang expert who works with police and at-risk youths. "It's easier to get a gun than it is to get a car."[37] When sixteen-year-old Luis Cosgaya-Alvarez wanted a gun, he simply bought one on the street from an illegal dealer. Less than two weeks later in Seattle, Washington, Cosgaya-Alvarez used the gun to shoot and kill a man with whom he was arguing.

## Socioeconomic Status

Teens who live in families and communities with low socioeconomic status have an increased risk of violence. Socioeconomic status is determined by education, income, and occupation. Teens from low socioeconomic backgrounds are more likely to show higher levels of aggression and hostility.

Family income is a strong predictor of violence. According to a 2010 study by the Substance Abuse and Mental Health Services Administration, violent behavior is more common for teens from families with low income than those from families with high income. Researchers interviewed teens between 2004 and 2008 and asked if they had participated in one or more violent behaviors in the past year: getting into a serious fight at school or work, taking part in a group-on-group fight, or attacking someone with the intent to hurt them. The study reported that more than 40 percent of teens who lived in families with an annual income of less than $20,000 engaged in at least one type of violent behavior. In comparison, only 24.6 percent of teens from families earning more than $75,000 in annual income participated in at least one violent activity.

**Teens from low socioeconomic backgrounds are more likely to show higher levels of aggression and hostility.**

Education also plays a role in socioeconomic status and violence. According to the American Psychological Association, children from abusive or neglectful homes are more likely to have lower levels of academic achievement. This is likely to result in their having lower incomes as adults, which increases their chances of becoming victims or perpetrators of violence. In addition, poor academic performance has also been linked to violent behavior in teens. In the 2010 National Survey on Drug Use and Health, researchers found that students with low grades were more likely to engage in violent behavior. Regardless of family income, more than 50 percent of teens with a "D" average or lower reported engaging in violent behavior as compared with 15 to 28 percent of teens with an "A" average in school.

Teens living in economically disadvantaged communities have a higher risk of engaging in violent behavior than other young people. These communities often have a high percentage of disrupted or single-parent families, which can lessen adult involvement with teens. These communities may also have limited after-school activities to provide a safe place for teens. Having nowhere to go and little adult supervision can increase opportunities for teens to get into trouble.

In addition, communities with adults who are involved in crime may increase a teen's risk of violence. Teens learn negative behavior from watching adults solve problems using violence. In addition, teens who are exposed to violence in their communities may feel helpless. To assert some control over their environment, teens may turn to violence themselves. They may carry a gun or knife or join a gang for protection. Some studies have found that teens are more likely to strike out violently if they face a perceived threat, wanting to make the first blow.

All of these factors, from community and family environment to individual characteristics and personality, influence teens as they decide whether to behave aggressively or to solve problems in a nonviolent way. And when a teen chooses violence, the underlying causes are sometimes not easily understood or identified. "You can't necessarily ascribe a set of root factors or behaviors to [a violent] event,"[38] says Staci Young, senior faculty director of Medical College of Wisconsin's Youth Violence Prevention Initiative.

# Primary Source Quotes*

## What Causes Teen Violence?

66 The big difference to me between today and previous generations is not kids, it's the opportunity and access that, you know, that they have to get their hands on guns. And so a lot of these fights, you know, that might have occurred as fistfights in the past now occur as shootings.99

—Lawrence Steinberg, interview by Michel Martin, "Teen Violence: Can It Be Prevented?," NPR, March 6, 2012. www.npr.org.

Steinberg, a professor of psychology at Temple University, has done extensive research on youth violence and psychological development during adolescence.

66 This work could hardly be more urgent. Today, we know that the majority of our young people—more than 60 percent of them—have been exposed to crime, abuse, and violence.99

—Eric Holder, speech presented at the National Forum on Youth Violence Prevention Summit, April 5, 2011. www.justice.gov.

Holder is attorney general of the United States.

* Editor's Note: While the definition of a primary source can be narrowly or broadly defined, for the purposes of Compact Research, a primary source consists of: 1) results of original research presented by an organization or researcher; 2) eyewitness accounts of events, personal experience, or work experience; 3) first-person editorials offering pundits' opinions; 4) government officials presenting political plans and/or policies; 5) representatives of organizations presenting testimony or policy.

Primary Source Quotes

66 Both teens who use violence and those who are vulnerable to being victimized have typically experienced previous victimizations, harsh parenting and other adversities. 99

—Sherry L. Hamby, "Teen Dating Violence Often Occurs Alongside Other Abuse," American Psychological Association, February 13, 2012. www.apa.org.

Hamby is a research associate professor at Sewanee, the University of the South, and a research associate with the University of New Hampshire Crimes Against Children Research Center.

66 Access to guns is a significant factor in American school shootings. If kids could not and did not bring guns to school, we wouldn't have Columbine, Virginia Tech or Chardon, Ohio. 99

—Frank Ochberg, "Why Does America Lead the World in School Shootings?," *Global Public Square*, CNN World, February 28, 2012. http://globalpublicsquare.blogs.cnn.com.

Ochberg is a clinical professor of psychiatry at Michigan State University and former associate director of the National Institute of Mental Health.

66 We know that exposure to violence—as a witness or a victim—can have devastating, long-term effects on our children—increasing their chances for depression, substance-abuse, and violent behavior. 99

—Eric Holder, speech presented at the National Forum on Youth Violence Prevention Summit, April 5, 2011. www.justice.gov.

Holder is attorney general of the United States.

66 The consequences of dating violence—spanning impaired development to physical harm—pose a threat to the health and well-being of teens across our Nation, and it is essential we come together to break the cycle of violence that burdens too many of our sons and daughters. 99

—Barack Obama, "Presidential Proclamation: National Teen Dating Violence Awareness and Prevention Month, 2012," January 31, 2012. www.whitehouse.gov.

Obama is the forty-fourth president of the United States.

**❝Kids who resort to crime and violence do so because criminal communities give them a network of support that they wouldn't otherwise find from their classmates or family members.❞**

—Jenny Lee, "Youth on Violence: Relearn What It Means to Fix Things," *Lexington Herald-Leader*, August 12, 2012. www.kentucky.com.

Lee is an eighteen-year-old freshman at the University of Chicago.

**❝Too many of our young people's lives are being taken far too early due to senseless and preventable gun violence.❞**

—E.J. Henderson, with R.T. Rybak, "Youth Violence Prevention in Minneapolis Moves Forward," City of Minneapolis, July 30, 2012. www.minneapolismn.gov.

Henderson is an NFL player involved in Minneapolis youth violence prevention efforts; Rybak is mayor of Minneapolis.

## What Causes Teen Violence?

- According to the National Survey on Drug Use and Health, **49.8 percent** of youths aged twelve to seventeen who used an illegal drug in the year prior to the survey engaged in violent behavior as compared with 26.6 percent of youth who did not use illegal drugs.

- **Twenty-seven percent** of teens who abused illicit drugs reported attacking someone with the intent to harm, reports the Office of National Drug Policy.

- Of youth homicide victims aged ten to twenty-four, **84 percent** were killed with a firearm, reports the CDC.

- According to SAMHSA's 2010 report *Violent Behaviors and Family Income in Adolescents*, **two-fifths of adolescents** surveyed between 2004 and 2008 who lived in families with income of less than $20,000 engaged in violent behavior within the previous year.

- According to the CDC, bullying behavior is more likely in teens who have **poor self-control**, who have been subjected to harsh parenting practices, and who see violence as an acceptable way to solve conflict.

- According to the CDC, the presence of **risk factors** does not always mean a teen will become violent.

- Teens who are involved in **gangs or drugs** are more likely to be the victims or perpetrators of teen violence than other teens, according to the Office of National Drug Policy.

## Violent Crime Arrests Higher Among Young Males

Young males are far more likely to be arrested for violent crimes than are females, according to statistics compiled by the Centers for Disease Control and Prevention. Among males, arrest rates for violent crime are highest in the 15- to 19-year-old age range, followed closely by young men between the ages of 20 and 24. Among females, arrests for violent crimes are most common among 20- to 24-year-olds followed closely by females between the ages of 15 and 19.

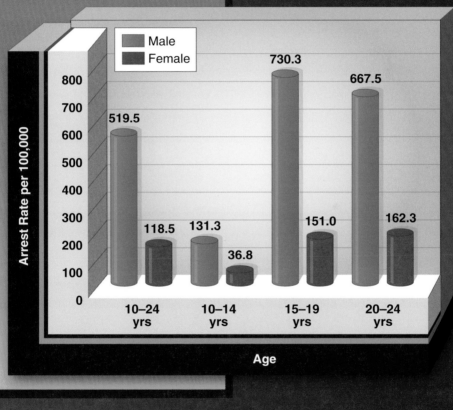

Source: Centers for Disease Control and Prevention, "Violent Crime Arrest Rates Among Persons Ages 10–24 Year, by Age and Sex, United States, 2009," April 15, 2011. www.cdc.gov.

- The **most dangerous time of day** for teens at risk of violence is just after-school gets out because many youth have no adult supervision during that period.

## Violent Behavior Among Adolescents, by Family Income

Violent behavior is more prevalent in adolescents from low-income families than from high-income families, according to the 2010 National Survey on Drug Use and Health. As the survey shows, 40.5 percent of adolescents from families with annual incomes of less than $20,000 engaged in at least one of three violent behaviors—a higher percentage than is shown for other income groups.

| Family Income | Got into a Serious Fight at School or Work (%) | Took Part in a Group-against-Group Fight (%) | Attacked Someone with the Intent to Hurt Them (%) | At Least One of Three Violent Behaviors (%) |
|---|---|---|---|---|
| **Total** | **22.6%** | **16.1%** | **7.6%** | **30.9%** |
| Family Income Less Than $20,000 | 30.6% | 21.5% | 11.2% | 40.5% |
| Family Income $20,000 to $49,999 | 24.9% | 17.9% | 8.8% | 33.8% |
| Family Income $50,000 to $74,999 | 20.0% | 14.2% | 6.7% | 27.8% |
| Family Income $75,000 or More | 17.4% | 12.6% | 5.1% | 24.6% |

Source: NSDUH Report, "Violent Behaviors and Family Income Among Adolescents," August 19, 2010. www.oas.samhsa.gov.

- Teens **without strong family ties**, positive peer influences, or commitment to school are more at risk of violence.

- According to the Office of National Drug Control Policy, teens who participate in gangs are more likely to **commit violent acts** and use drugs.

- Gang membership has reached **14 to 30 percent** of the population in many urban areas, reports the CDC.

- Researchers at Indiana University report that children living with high-conflict parents are more likely to see **aggression** as a good way to solve problems.

## Violent Behavior and Grades

Violent behaviors occur in youth of all backgrounds, but youth with lower grades in school have a significantly higher rate of violence. In a 2010 report by the Substance Abuse and Mental Health Services Administration, among adolescents aged 12 to 17 who attended school in the past year, students with a "D" average or lower were three times more likely to participate in violent behaviors than students with an "A" average. Violent behavior in the study was defined as getting into a serious fight at school or work, participating in a group-against-group fight, or attacking others with the intent to hurt them seriously.

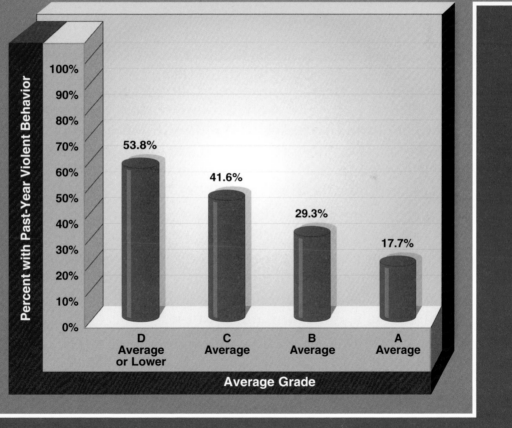

Source: NSDUH Report, "Violent Behaviors and Family Income among Adolescents," August 19, 2010. www.oas.samhsa.gov.

- Teens who are **engaged with their family** and community are less likely to turn to violence and drugs, says the Office of National Drug Policy.

# How Do Media Influence Teen Violence?

66There are some key impacts of violent media on children that are very well demonstrated in research. They include increases in the likelihood of aggressive behavior, increases in desensitization to violence and an increase in the overall view that the world is more scary and hostile than it really is.99

—Wayne Warburton, deputy director, Macquarie University Children and Families Research Centre.

66In my own research, correlations between media violence and aggression are usually due to underlying family violence or personality issues. At most, media violence is a symptom, not a cause.99

—Christopher Ferguson, assistant professor of psychology, Texas A&M International University.

The media can be a powerful influence in developing values and shaping behaviors for children and teens. Today's teens are surrounded by media more than any previous generation. Teens watch television shows on demand, stream movies onto tablet computers, and download music instantly onto mp3 players.

With teens having such easy access to media, many adults are worried about the effect media has on youth. Some adults believe that violent images encourage violent and aggressive behavior. "The biggest misconception is that it's harmless entertainment," says Vic Strasburger, a professor of pediatrics at the University of New Mexico School of Medicine. Strasburger has written extensively about the effects of media on children. "Media are one of the most powerful teachers of children that we know of."[39]

## Rising Media Consumption

Today's youth are exposed to more media than previous generations. According to the Kaiser Family Foundation, youth in 2009 averaged ten hours, forty-five minutes of media exposure in a typical day compared with approximately seven hours, thirty minutes a decade earlier, in 1999. Within the hours of media exposure, youth spend the most time watching television. According to the Parents Television Council, American youth spend an average of four hours per day watching television. In addition to television, youth are exposed to media when listening to music, using computers, playing video games, reading books, and watching movies.

New technology has made it easier for young people to access media in all forms. DVDs, DVRs, and on-demand programming are joined by Internet broadcasts and other online entertainment streamed on tablet computers, laptops, and cell phones. "They're using all the technology available in their households," says Patricia McDonough, a senior vice president of insights analysis and policy at Nielsen Company, a global market research firm. "They're using the DVD, they're on the Internet. They're not giving up any media—they're just picking up more."[40]

> " Today's teens are surrounded by media more than any previous generation. "

In addition, there are more choices for today's youth, as a larger portion of programming is targeted specifically at them. Television channels such as the Disney Channel, MTV, Nickelodeon, and Cartoon Network broadcast shows aimed at children and teens twenty-four hours a day, seven days a week. "When I was a kid, I had Saturday morning cartoons," McDonough says. "And now there are programs they want to watch available to them whenever they want to watch them."[41]

## Violence on Television

As young people watch more television, they are also watching more violence. According to the American Academy of Pediatrics (AAP), young people who watch three to four hours of noneducational television daily will have seen about eight thousand murders by the time they finish elementary school. By age twelve, the average adolescent has witnessed tens of thousands acts of violence.

Even shows for the youngest viewers feature violence. Cartoon characters use violence to solve problems. Shows such as *Power Rangers*, *Star Wars*, *Spider-Man*, and *Looney Tunes* feature characters that fight or flee from violence and who celebrate violent acts. Many more cartoons use over-the-top violence to keep youth interested and watching. The American Academy of Pediatrics warns that repeated exposure to media violence may desensitize children to violence and put them at risk of growing up to become violent teens. "Extensive research evidence indicates that media violence can contribute to aggressive behavior, desensitization to violence, nightmares, and fear of being harmed,"[42] the AAP says in a policy statement on media violence.

## Movie Violence

The movie industry recognizes that some violent images and themes may be too mature for developing adolescents. For this reason, every movie receives a rating from the Motion Picture Association of America. These ratings warn parents and youth that the content of the movie, including its level of violence, may be too mature for younger viewers. The ratings are intended to act as a deterrent, stopping minors from watching films with graphic violence.

> " Repeated exposure to violent images can cause youth to become immune to the horror of violence. "

Yet in a paper published in 2008 in the journal *Pediatrics*, Dartmouth researchers reported that, nonetheless, young adolescents aged ten to fourteen were regularly being exposed to graphic violence in R-rated movies. They found that an average of 12.5 percent of youth in this age group viewed these violent movies. *Scary Movie*, an R-rated film, was seen by an estimated 10 million youth, or about 48 percent of ten to fourteen-year-olds. "Our data reveal a disturbingly high rate of exposure among 10–14 year olds nationally to extremely violent movies,"says Keilah Worth, the lead author on the study. "The R rating in this country is clearly not preventing our young people from seeing them."[43]

## Effects of Viewing Violence

Experts with several organizations including the American Medical Association believe that extensive viewing of television and movie violence causes greater aggressiveness in youth. Repeated exposure to violent images can cause youth to become immune to the horror of violence. They may mirror violent behavior and gradually accept violence as a way to solve problems and conflicts.

Some studies show that media violence can have a powerful effect on a teen's developing mind and value system. Researchers at the University of Michigan concluded in a 2009 study that watching violent television as a child can lead to aggressive behavior as a teen and adult. The study followed 320 children into adulthood. Researchers found that men who had scored in the top 20 percent on childhood exposure to television violence were twice as likely to have pushed, grabbed, or shoved their wives in a one-year period. Women in the top 20 percent were also more violent. "They report having punched, beaten or choked another adult at over four times the rate of women who were not exposed to media violence,"[44] says Jeff McIntyre of the American Psychological Association.

> " Violent games can increase thoughts of violence and make teens more likely to argue with others. "

Yet other research finds that the link between media violence and teen violence is weak. In a study published in 2010, assistant professor of psychology Christopher Ferguson from Texas A&M International University concluded that media violence was not related to serious acts of youth aggression and violence. In the study, Ferguson followed 302 mainly Hispanic youth between the ages of ten and fourteen. He found that exposure to violence from video games or television did not predict aggressive behavior in these youth in the following year. Instead, Ferguson found that depression more strongly predicted aggressive behavior.

## Violent Video Games

Some of today's most popular video games, such as *Call of Duty* and *Halo*, arm players with machine guns and other deadly weapons. Teens playing these games prowl the game landscape in search of other players and characters to gun down, earning points for each kill. Each year, video game graphics become more realistic as they reward acts of violence and aggression.

Several experts and parent groups worry that extreme violence in these games might lead to increased teen aggression and violence in the real world. Psychologists Douglas A. Gentile and Craig A. Anderson from Iowa State University have been studying the effects of the games for more than thirty years. "[We] found consistent evidence that violent games increase desensitization [and] aggressive thoughts, feelings, physiology, and behaviors and decrease helpful behaviors,"[45] they say.

Playing violent video games can affect a teen's aggression in several ways. Violent games can increase thoughts of violence and make teens more likely to argue with others. Watching repeated violent acts on the screen, teens may also become desensitized to violence around them, real or imaginary. Experts also say that teens who play violent video games demonstrate increased aggressive behavior immediately following a game session. These behavioral changes may arise because of neurological changes that occur when playing the game.

> In 2011 the American Psychological Association reported that competitiveness may be a more significant factor than violence in aggressive behavior.

Some experts believe that violent video games can have an even stronger impact on teens than violence in television or movies. Watching a TV show or movie is a passive activity. In a video game, a teen becomes an active participant, seeking to kill or harm other players. The shooting skills used in some violent games can carry over into the real world. The

US Marine Corp, US Army, and many law enforcement agencies use shooting video games to train recruits on firearms. In Kentucky, a school shooter may have used video game skills to hunt down his victims. "The 14-year-old killer in the Paducah, Kentucky, school shooting had never fired a real pistol in his life. Nevertheless he fired eight shots, five of them head shots, the other three upper torso shots, killing eight children. Where did he get the skill and [the] will to kill? Most likely from violent video games and media violence,"[46] writes Ofer Zur.

## Violence in the Media Linked to Brain Changes

Some researchers are investigating whether there is a biological link between violence in the media and aggressive behavior. Some believe that exposure to media violence triggers unintended changes in the brain. These changes may increase a young person's aggressive tendencies or lower inhibitions, which may lead to antisocial or aggressive behavior.

In Indianapolis, a 2010 study by researchers at the Indiana University School of Medicine tested the effects of violent video games on the brains of healthy males, aged eighteen to twenty-nine. The study subjects were split into two groups. The first group played a shooting video game for one week, and then did not play it the second week. The second group of test subjects did not play the violent game at all during the two-week period. After one week of violent game play, group one subjects showed changes in brain regions that were associated with cognitive function and emotional control. These changes were reduced after the second week of the study, when the subjects did not play the violent game. "For the first time, we have found that a sample of randomly assigned young adults showed less activation in certain frontal brain regions following a week of playing violent video games at home," says Yang Wang, assistant research professor in the Department of Radiology and Imaging Sciences at the university. "These brain regions are important for controlling emotion and aggressive behavior."[47]

## Challenge to Link between Video Games and Violence

Several experts, including Ferguson, argue that the studies of media violence and youth are flawed and do not prove cause and effect. Ferguson also points out that serious violent crimes among youth have decreased since 1996, while at the same time video game sales and use have increased. "Although there are some studies that find links between violent games and mild forms of aggression, there are also studies which find no evidence for any links at all. I've found . . . no evidence of harmful video game or television violence effects,"[48] says Ferguson.

Other researchers challenge the link between violent video games and school shootings. Many of the perpetrators of these extremely violent crimes displayed characteristics such as anger, psychosis, and aggression. These characteristics made them more likely to become violent whether or not they played video games or watched violent television shows. Experts contend that the presence of these strong predictors of violence make it difficult to charge video games with being a direct cause of youth violence.

In 2011 the American Psychological Association reported that competitiveness may be a more significant factor than violence in aggressive behavior. In a series of studies, researchers found that video game violence by itself did not increase aggressive behavior. Rather, they discovered that players who played more competitive games exhibited higher levels of aggressive behavior, no matter how much violence was in the game. "These findings suggest that the level of competitiveness in video games is an important factor in the relation between video games and aggressive behavior, with highly competitive games leading to greater elevations in aggression than less competitive games,"[49] writes lead author Paul J.C. Adachi, a researcher in the Department of Psychology at Brock University in Canada.

The level of violence in the media concerns many adults. While several studies have suggested a connection between media violence and teen aggression, it remains unclear how much of an effect media violence has on teens and their behavior. According to the Southern California Academic Center of Excellence on Youth Violence Prevention at the University of California, Riverside, "translation of these findings to the 'real' world has been problematic."[50] For this reason, many people believe more research is needed.

# Primary Source Quotes*

# How Do Media Influence Teen Violence?

> 66 Psychological studies purporting to show a connection between exposure to violent video games and harmful effects on children do not prove that such exposure causes minors to act aggressively. 99

—Antonin Scalia, majority opinion, *Brown vs. Entertainment Merchants Association*, June 27, 2011. www.supremecourt.gov.

Scalia is a US Supreme Court justice.

> 66 It is time for the public health establishment to accept the fact that playing violent video games increases the 'risk' that the player will behave more aggressively. 99

—L. Rowell Huesmann, "Nailing the Coffin Shut on Doubts That Violent Video Games Stimulate Aggression: Comment on Andersen et al.," *Psychological Bulletin 2010*, vol 136, no. 2, pp. 179–181. http://rcgd.isr.umich.edu.

Huesmann is the Amos N. Tversky Collegiate Professor of Communication Studies and Psychology at the University of Michigan.

Primary Source Quotes

Bracketed quotes indicate conflicting positions.

* Editor's Note: While the definition of a primary source can be narrowly or broadly defined, for the purposes of Compact Research, a primary source consists of: 1) results of original research presented by an organization or researcher; 2) eyewitness accounts of events, personal experience, or work experience; 3) first-person editorials offering pundits' opinions; 4) government officials presenting political plans and/or policies; 5) representatives of organizations presenting testimony or policy.

66 Violent tendencies reside within the personality, whether or not the person watches programming depicting violence. The television program, the movie, or the videogame do not turn him into something alien to his basic personality. 99

—Stanton Samenow, "Watching Violence in the Media Does Not Cause Crime," *Psychology Today*, February 24, 2012. www.psychologytoday.com.

Samenow is a clinical psychologist practicing in Alexandria, Virginia, and author of *Inside the Criminal Mind*.

66 Violent games increase aggressive attitudes and behaviors, both immediately and over long periods of time. 99

—Craig Anderson and Douglas Gentile, "Don't Read More Into the Supreme Court's Ruling on California Video Game Law," Iowa State University, June 30, 2011. www.psychology.iastate.edu

Anderson is a distinguished professor of psychology and Gentile is an associate professor of child psychology at Iowa State University: they are two of the coauthors of *Violent Video Game Effects on Children and Adolescents*.

66 There is a culture of violence among our youth. With the violent movies and violent video games that gives points for the best shot and the music that promotes using a handgun to settle conflict or handle frustration. 99

—Dorothy Johnson-Speight, testimony before the House Judiciary Committee, Subcommittee on Crime, Terrorism, and Homeland Security: "Youth Violence: Trends, Myths, and Solutions," February 11, 2009, p. 7. http://judiciary.house.gov.

Johnson-Speight is the founder of Mothers In Charge and mother of a murdered youth.

66 Put bluntly, the scientific belief that video game violence causes youth violence, serious aggression, or brain damage is falsified. 99

—Christopher J. Ferguson, "Violence in Video Games: Advocating for the Wrong Cause?," *The Advocate*, Spring 2012. p. 18. www.apa.org.

Ferguson is an associate professor of psychology at Texas A&M International University.

**❝I think we should be concerned about violent content in cartoons in terms of the potential effect.❞**

—Andrew J. Weaver in "New Study Finds That Violence Doesn't Add to Children's Enjoyment of TV Shows, Movies," Indiana University, May 24, 2011. http://newsinfo.iu.edu/news/page/normal/18672.html

Weaver is an assistant professor of telecommunications in Indiana University's College of Arts and Sciences.

......................................................................................................................................................

**❝The depiction of violence in the media simply isn't realistic. It offers a glamorized version of the truth, omitting all of the legal details that follow and all of the consequences for the aggressor.❞**

—Michael Gomez, "Youth on Violence: No One Pays for Violence on Reality TV Shows," *Lexington Herald-Leader*, August 12, 2012. www.kentucky.com.

Gomez is a seventeen-year-old high school senior at Bryan Station High School in Lexington, Kentucky.

......................................................................................................................................................

# How Do Media Influence Teen Violence?

- The American Academy of Pediatrics reports that by age eighteen, the average young American will have viewed about **two hundred thousand acts of violence** on television, which may increase their risk of violent or aggressive behavior.

- According to the American Psychological Association, children will watch as many as **eight thousand murders** in the media by the time they finish elementary school at age eleven, desensitizing them to violence as teens.

- According to the ACT for Strong Families program, youth under age six spend a daily average of two hours with a television and DVD player, one hour with video games, and fifty minutes with a computer, which may also increase their exposure to media violence.

- American youth watch an average of **four thousand hours of TV** before they enter kindergarten, exposing them to thousands of acts of violence.

- Youth are exposed to twenty to **twenty-five acts of violence** per hour on Saturday morning TV programs according to the American Academy of Family Physicians.

- **Twenty-three percent** of parents say their children have imitated aggressive behavior seen on TV, such as hitting or kicking, reports the Kaiser Family Foundation.

## Exposure to Media's Violent Content Is Increasing

The amount of media exposure for young people aged eight to eighteen has increased over a ten-year period. In 1999 the average youth was exposed to more than seven hours of media daily. Ten years later, in 2009, the average youth had nearly eleven hours of media exposure per day. Experts worry about heightened exposure, in particular, because content has become more violent over time.

**Media Exposure, over Time**
Among all 8- to 18-year-olds, total amount
of media exposure in a typical day:

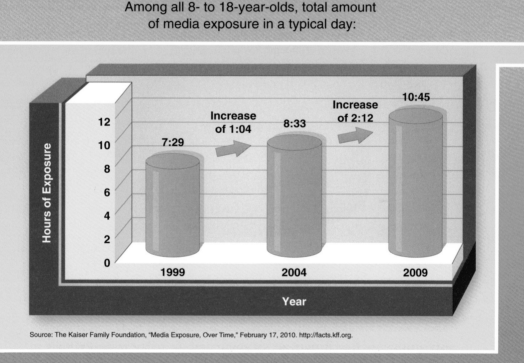

Source: The Kaiser Family Foundation, "Media Exposure, Over Time," February 17, 2010. http://facts.kff.org.

- The Pew Research Center reports that **97 percent** of youths aged twelve to seventeen played some type of video game and that two-thirds of them played action and adventure games that contain violent content.

- Functional MRI brain scans found that **brain areas** in teens that control aggression became less active after watching violent movies.

## Movie and Television Violence Lead to Societal Violence

In a July 2012 national telephone survey of one thousand American adults, a majority expressed the view that violent movies and television programs lead to more violence in society. The survey was conducted shortly after the deadly Aurora, Colorado, shooting at a midnight screening of the newest *Batman* film.

### Percent of Adults Surveyed Who Believe Violence in Movies and Television Leads to Violence in Society

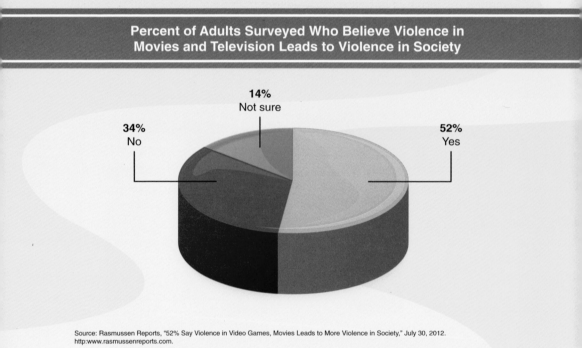

**14%**
Not sure

**34%**
No

**52%**
Yes

Source: Rasmussen Reports, "52% Say Violence in Video Games, Movies Leads to More Violence in Society," July 30, 2012. http:www.rasmussenreports.com.

- According to the American Academy of Pediatrics, **38 percent** of youth reported exposure to violence online.

- The Kaiser Family Foundation reports that nearly **two out of three television shows** watched by teens contain some violence, averaging about **six violent acts per hour.**

- Dartmouth researchers report that an average of **12.5 percent** of youth aged ten to fourteen watch R-rated, violent movies.

# Violence and Top-Selling Video Games

According to sales data from the Entertainment Software Association, 7 out of 10 of the top-selling video games sold in 2011 were rated T (teen, for 13 and older) or M (mature, for 17 and older). The Entertainment Software Rating Board says T-rated titles "may contain violence, suggestive themes, crude humor, minimal blood, simulated gambling, and/or infrequent use of strong language." M-rated titles "may contain intense violence, blood and gore, sexual content and/or strong language." When all 20 of the top-selling video games are considered, however, only 9 have T or M ratings while the rest are rated acceptable for younger ages, either 6 and older or 10 and older.

| Top Selling Video Games of 2011 | | |
|---|---|---|
| Rank | Title | ESRB Rating |
| 1 | Call of Duty: Modern Warfare 3 | Mature |
| 2 | Just Dance 3 | Everyone 10+ |
| 3 | Madden NFL 12 | Everyone |
| 4 | Elder Scrolls V: Skyrim | Mature |
| 5 | Battlefield 3 | Mature |
| 6 | Call of Duty: Black Ops | Mature |
| 7 | Batman:Arkham City | Teen |
| 8 | Gears of War 3 | Mature |
| 9 | Just Dance 2 | Everyone |
| 10 | Assassin's Creed: Revelations | Mature |
| 11 | Pokémon White Version | Everyone |
| 12 | Zumba Fitness: Join the Party | Everyone |
| 13 | NBA 2K12 | Everyone |
| 14 | Lego Star Wars III: The Clone Wars | Everyone 10+ |
| 15 | Pokémon Black Version | Everyone |
| 16 | NBA 2K11 | Everyone |
| 17 | Mortal Kombat 2011 | Mature |
| 18 | Michael Jackson the Experience | Everyone 10+ |
| 19 | NCAA Football 12 | Everyone |
| 20 | L.A. Noire | Mature |

Source: Entertainment Software Association, "2012 Sales, Demographic, and Usage Data: Essential Facts about the Computer and Video Game Industry," 2012, p. 9. www.theesa.com.

# Can Teen Violence Be Stopped?

66We must engage directly with our children, starting at the youngest age, and must engage with them at every stage of their lives and teach them that violence doesn't solve anything, and that respect for others is the foundation for a safe and healthy society.99

—Arne Duncan, US Secretary of Education.

66We need a comprehensive, coordinated approach to address today's youth violence, one that encompasses the latest research and the freshest approaches.99

—Eric Holder, US Attorney General.

The best solution to ending teen violence is to stop the violence before it begins—before a young person even reaches adolescence. Accomplishing that goal is not easy, because the factors leading to teen violence are both varied and individual. Still many people believe that teen violence can be stopped. Sergeant Mike Cross, who works for the Topeka, Kansas, police department, regularly deals with violent teens. He believes that intervention efforts can have a positive effect on teen violence. "They are all preventable incidents,"[51] he says.

Experts agree that to achieve long-lasting change, prevention efforts should focus on eliminating the factors that put teens at risk for violence. Successful violence prevention also promotes strong families and safe after-school activities as ways to protect teens at risk for violence.

## Early Intervention Is Critical

For violence prevention to be most effective, early intervention is critical. Experts say that children learn at an early age how to deal with conflict. Research has shown that when children are exposed to violence at a young age, they learn to model violent behavior. Early prevention programs aim to reduce violence that young children experience and replace it with healthy ways to deal with conflict.

One successful early intervention program is the SNAP (Stop Now and Plan) program. SNAP teaches children and adults how to deal effectively with anger. SNAP coaches youth in methods to control impulses and resolve conflicts. "I think it has done an amazing job in teaching them how to use self-control and to slow down and think about their actions and the consequences to their actions,"[52] says Cory Kunicky, a guidance counselor in Pittsburgh, whose students have participated in SNAP.

A group of young girls in a Pittsburgh SNAP program say the program has taught them to recognize anger before they react to it. In one therapy session, the girls analyzed the signals their body sends when they get angry. Some girls reported their hands ball up, their hearts race, their faces turn red, and their bodies shake. "Once they understand what is happening, they can do something specific to calm themselves down,"[53] says Brandi Hudson, SNAP program coordinator at the Holy Family Institute in Pittsburgh.

## Improve Social Skills

Violence often results from conflicts between people. Therefore, teaching a teen positive social skills and nonviolent ways to resolve conflicts can be an important tool for violence prevention. These programs attempt to reduce antisocial and aggressive behaviors by developing these skills.

In one program, researchers at Duke University's Center for Child and Family Policy randomly assigned kindergartners at risk for chronic violence to a program that helped them learn how to manage impulses and negotiate disputes. Following the children into young adulthood, the researchers reported that those who had learned these social skills reported fewer emergency room visits for violence-related injuries. This group also reported a 48 percent reduction in arrests for severe violence as compared with those children who did not receive the social skills training.

## Positive Relationships

Research has shown that positive relationships with parents, friends, romantic partners, and other adults can be protective factors against violence. Protective factors help teens resist or avoid violent behavior. One of the most important relationships in a teen's life is with one or both parents. This relationship can be a powerful protective factor for a teen to avoid violence. Family counseling is one way families improve communication and strengthen the parent-child bond.

Yet many youth at risk for violence come from fractured families, in which one or both parents are not around. In these cases, adult mentors can become positive role models. In Baltimore, Maryland, thirty-four-year-old Tard Carter is a violence interrupter with Operation Safe Streets, a program that hires ex-convicts to intervene in potentially violent situations, such as in neighborhoods where gangs are active. As a convicted felon, Carter uses his past experiences to talk to youth about drugs and violence. He also intervenes when street violence begins to spiral out of control. In one instance, Carter watched as two teens from rival gangs began to argue. When one drew a gun, he ran and stopped the shooter before he fired. "I was like, 'Hey, stop. Chill. You don't wanna do that,'"[54] Carter says. Although one boy ran off, Carter talked to the other, calmed him and reminded him that a moment of rage could land him in jail.

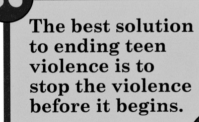

**The best solution to ending teen violence is to stop the violence before it begins.**

With the help of Carter and the Safe Streets program, juvenile involvement in homicides in Baltimore has declined over a three-year period. By stopping one killing, the program also stops retaliatory killing and violence. "Stopping one homicide through mediation could buy you peace for months down the road,"[55] says professor Daniel Webster, codirector of the Johns Hopkins Center for Gun Policy and Research.

Learning how to build positive relationships with romantic partners can also reduce teen violence. Launched in 2010, the Tina Project is working to educate students and school employees about dating violence and its prevention. The Tina Project is named after teenager Tina

Croucher, who was shot and killed by an abusive ex-boyfriend in 1992 in southern Ohio. The project uses in-school workshops to talk to teens and teachers about healthy relationships and how to recognize the red flags of an unhealthy relationship. It also provides crisis intervention and support services to teens who have experienced dating violence.

## Community-Based Prevention

Many communities seek to involve neighborhood residents in antiviolence efforts. They do this through educational programs that raise awareness about teen violence and its impact on neighborhoods. One community program, CeaseFire, uses public education slogans such as "Don't shoot. I want to grow up," to raise awareness in more than twenty American cities. It also mobilizes communities to get involved in helping teens resolve conflicts. CeaseFire's tactics are working. In 2009 the US Department of Justice found after a three-year review that several Illinois communities using CeaseFire had reduced shootings between 16 and 34 percent.

Because many instances of violence occur after school when there is little supervision of adolescents, some communities have opened after-school centers and programs. These centers engage youth and give them a safe place to go.

## Schools Taking Precautions

Many schools are taking precautions to keep students safe. To keep weapons away from school property, some schools conduct random locker searches and bag checks. They limit school entry and exit points, keeping each under teacher or administrator supervision. Other schools have installed metal detectors, making every student and visitor pass through the detectors as they enter the school building.

Schools are also fighting teen violence through education and prevention programs. Many have added conflict resolution lessons and workshops to the school curriculum. Peer programs educate students about the warning signs of violence. Under the Safe School Ambassadors program, school staff train student ambassadors—typically leaders of various cliques who can help stop minor bullying and aggression before it escalates. According to Kevin Crider, a counselor at Los Angeles' Gardena High School, an ambassador was able to prevent escalating violence after a series of racial brawls at the school. The student spotted a teen with a gun in his locker and reported it to school police. The police arrested the teen before any additional violence erupted.

Despite these efforts, some people believe that schools are not doing enough. "Relatively few schools . . . are putting into action the strategies we know are important for preventing violence,"[56] says Shane Jimerson, school psychology professor at the University of California at Santa Barbara. For example, a 2012 study published in the journal *Pediatrics* found that a majority of high schools do not have procedures or trained staff to deal with dating violence. Less than half of the schools surveyed taught students about dating violence or had information posted around the school. In addition, about 70 percent of US high school counselors have not received any formal training in dating-violence counseling. The study's lead author, Jagdish Khubchandani, an assistant professor of community health at Ball State University in Muncie, Indiana, believes the findings highlight a significant problem. "For example, if a female is abused in a relationship in a high school and they go to a school counselor, the counselor would not have a set protocol or procedure to handle the problem,"[57] he says.

> " **Early prevention programs aim to reduce violence that young children experience and to replace it with healthy ways to deal with conflict.** "

## Some Programs Are Ineffective

Despite organizers' good intentions, not all violence prevention programs are effective. Research has shown that ineffective violence prevention programs include boot camps, gun buybacks, peer counseling, neighborhood watches, and home detention with electronic monitoring. Not only are these programs ineffective at preventing violence, they also waste scarce taxpayer dollars.

Scared Straight programs typically bring at-risk youth into an adult prison where they are confronted by inmates about the consequences of crime and violence—and see prison life firsthand. These programs attempt to scare teens into better behavior by showing them the potential consequences if they continue to act violently. Scared Straight programs are popular because they line up with a widely held community view—that getting tough on crime is one of the best ways to reduce youth violence.

Yet research has shown that these types of programs may do more harm than good. Studies have discovered that teen participants were up to 28 percent more likely to commit crimes than youth who did not participate in the programs. In addition, a number of program participants reported that the adult inmates sexually propositioned them or tried to steal their personal belongings. As a result of these findings, the Office of Juvenile Justice and Delinquency Prevention denounced Scared Straight programs in August 2011 and halted federal funding.

## Regulation of Media Violence

Some people have called for the government to increase regulation of violence in the media. Currently, the entertainment industry self-regulates and posts ratings on movies, television shows, video games, and music lyrics. Many people criticize this system, noting that it does not prevent young people from viewing violent content. For example, there are no restrictions on young teens purchasing violent video games that are rated "M" or mature for violent content.

Some states have proposed laws that regulate the sale of violent video games. In 2005 California passed a law that prohibited the sale of M-rated video games to minors. Advocates of the law claimed that it protects youth from the harmful effects of video game violence.

> " Research has shown that having positive relationships with parents, friends, romantic partners, and other adults can be a protective factor against violence. "

Opponents of the law argued that there is no scientific link between violent games and teen violence. They believe that deciding whether a teen should have access to violent content is the parent's responsibility, not the government's. In a nationwide October 2010 Gallup survey of one thousand thirty-three adults aged eighteen and older, 86 percent said that parents should have a good deal of responsibility in deciding which video games youth may buy or rent. At the same time, only

28 percent said that the government should have greater responsibility.

In 2011 the Supreme Court ruled against the California law in a 7-2 decision. The majority of the justices found that the California law violated the First Amendment right to free speech. "Like the protected books, plays and movies that preceded them, video games communicate ideas—and even social messages—through many familiar literary devices (such as characters, dialogue, plot and music) and through features distinctive to the medium (such as the player's interaction with the virtual world). That suffices to confer First Amendment protection,"[58] said Supreme Court justice Antonin Scalia in writing the majority opinion of the court. He also said that parents, not the government, should decide what games their children play. Within the court, Justice Stephen Breyer dissented. "What sense does it make to forbid selling to a 13-year-old boy a magazine with an image of a nude woman while protecting a sale to that 13-year-old of an interactive video game in which he actively, but virtually, binds and gags the woman, then tortures and kills her?,"[59] Breyer asked.

> Some states have proposed laws that regulate the sale of violent video games.

## Prevention Can Be Effective

With hard work and the proper approach, most experts believe, teen violence can be reduced and prevented. Whether at the individual, family, community, school, or governmental level, there is hope for teens in need.

Research suggests that prevention programs that feature positive role models and reinforcement are more effective than programs that scare with negative role models. "We all have to help [young people] process anger," says Father Michael L. Pfleger, Chicago activist and community leader. "We have to teach in our schools, in our families and in our churches, conflict resolution. . . . You have to understand that we've taught violence. We've taught it through TV. We've taught it through videos. . . . So we've taught—as a nation—violence. Now we have to teach nonviolence."[60]

# Can Teen Violence Be Stopped?

66 **Parents are important role models for teens (whether it seems like it or not) and also need to make sure their own relationships are respectful and egalitarian.**99

—Sherry L. Hamby, "Teen Dating Violence Often Occurs Alongside Other Abuse," American Psychological Association, February 13, 2012. www.apa.org.

Hamby is a research associate professor at Sewanee, the University of the South, and a research associate with the University of New Hampshire Crimes Against Children Research Center.

66 **We need more stories in the media about how young people have worked out conflict without the use of violence because that way you can begin the process of unlearning violent behavior.**99

—Tio Hardiman, interview by Michel Martin, "Teen Violence: Can It Be Prevented?" NPR, March 6, 2012. www.npr.org.

Hardiman is the Illinois director for CeaseFire.

Bracketed quotes indicate conflicting positions.

* Editor's Note: While the definition of a primary source can be narrowly or broadly defined, for the purposes of Compact Research, a primary source consists of: 1) results of original research presented by an organization or researcher; 2) eyewitness accounts of events, personal experience, or work experience; 3) first-person editorials offering pundits' opinions; 4) government officials presenting political plans and/or policies; 5) representatives of organizations presenting testimony or policy.

**❝The teenagers who are engaging in crime and violence are troubled; they need people in their lives who truly think about their well-being without acting condescending or criticizing . . . these kids need a real friend—one who can serve as a relatable role model.❞**

—Jenny Lee, "Youth on Violence: Relearn What It Means to Fix Things," *Lexington Herald-Leader*, August 12, 2012. www.kentucky.com.

Lee is an eighteen-year-old freshman at the University of Chicago.

**❝It's important to tell teens—girls and boys alike—from an early age that they have the power to get help and prevent others from being subjected to violence.❞**

—Felicia Laks, "Youth on Violence: Teach Teens to Recognize Abusive Behavior Signs," *Lexington Herald-Leader*, August 12, 2012. www.kentucky.com.

Laks is a sixteen-year-old Spanish immersion student at Bryan Station High School in Lexington, Kentucky.

**❝By intervening early we can change the trajectory, change the path that kids are on. Reduce the likelihood that they'll become affiliated with gangs, reduce the likelihood then of gang violence.❞**

—Tom Simon, "Preventing Kids from Gang-Joining: Collaboration Matters," National Institute for Justice, October 14, 2011 (CDC video). http://nij.ncjrs.gov.

Simon is with the Division of Violence Prevention at the CDC's National Center for Injury Prevention and Control in Atlanta, Georgia.

**❝Youth violence is a tough issue that requires the full community to respond if we want to effectively address it.❞**

—Tonya Allen in "Youth Violence Prevention Initiative Gets Lift," The Skillman Foundation, August 9, 2012. www.skillman.org.

Allen is an executive with the Skillman Foundation, a private philanthropy group that works to create safe schools and neighborhoods for youth.

**❝Safe communities begin with safe youth. And ensuring the safety of youth begins in the neighborhoods where they live, learn, work, and play.❞**

—Mariko Lockheart, "A Message from the Director of the Initiative," *Safe Youth, Safe Community*, Seattle Youth Violence Prevention Initiative, 2011, p. 3. www.seattle.gov.

Lockheart is the director of the Seattle Youth Violence Prevention Initiative.

**❝Ending youth violence is not something government can do on its own. That's why we're working to put more information in the hands of families, schools and communities.❞**

—Kathleen Sebelius, speech presented at the National Forum on Youth Violence Prevention, Washington, DC, April 2, 2012. www.hhs.gov.

Sebelius is the secretary of the US Department of Health and Human Services.

# Can Teen Violence Be Stopped?

- According to UCAN's 2012 National Teen Gun Survey, **76 percent** of teens nationwide believe that young people would benefit from more violence prevention programs.

- Communities using a CeaseFire violence intervention program reduced shootings between **16 and 34 percent**.

- School antibullying programs such as the Olweus Bullying Prevention Program can reduce incidents of school bullying by **50 percent** or more.

- According to a Duke University study, young adults who were taught social skills and conflict management in kindergarten experienced a **48 percent** reduction in arrests for severe violence.

- **Seventy percent** of US high school counselors have not received any formal training in dating-violence counseling.

- Participants in Scared Straight programs were up to **28 percent** more likely to offend than youth who did not participate in the programs.

- In a Gallup survey conducted in 2010, **86 percent** of respondents said parents should have a "great deal" of responsibility in deciding whether a child can buy or rent violent video games.

# Youth Homicide Rates Declining

Over a seventeen-year period, youth homicide rates for both males and females have declined, although males aged ten to twenty-four consistently had a significantly higher homicide rate than males and females of all ages. Experts say that the decline in youth homicide shows that prevention efforts such as early intervention, mentoring programs, and after-school programs are working. Still, more prevention efforts are needed to reduce homicide rates even further, especially for high-risk males.

## Trends in Homicide Rates Among Persons Aged 10–24 Years, by Sex, United States, 1991–2007

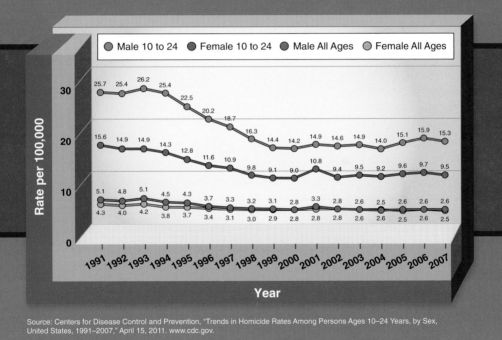

Source: Centers for Disease Control and Prevention, "Trends in Homicide Rates Among Persons Ages 10–24 Years, by Sex, United States, 1991–2007," April 15, 2011. www.cdc.gov.

- According to the *2011 Indicators of School Crime and Safety* report, **11 percent** of youth aged twelve to eighteen reported the use of metal detectors at their school.

# Violent Crime at School Declines

School violence peaked in 1993 with a rate of 42 homicides and 13 serious violent crimes per every 1,000 students in primary and secondary school. By 2010, these rates had declined to two homicides and four violent crimes per 1,000 students. Experts say that this decline is a result of a nationwide decline in violent crime at all age levels and the success of youth violence prevention programs.

## Homicides in Schools

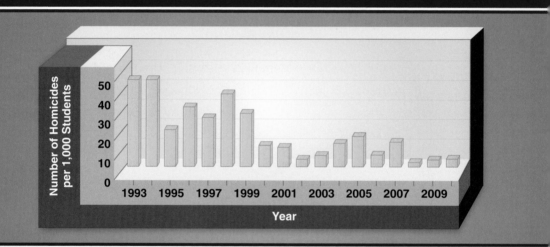

## Other Violent Crimes

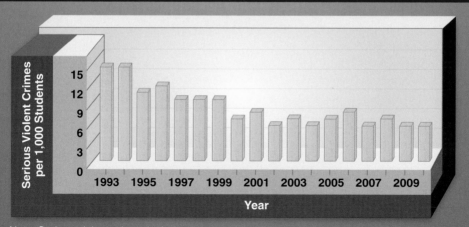

Note: Serious violent crimes include rape, sexual assault, robbery, and aggravated assault.

Source: Scott Neuman, "Violence in Schools: How Big a Problem Is It?," NPR.org, March 16, 2012. www.npr.org.

- According to the US Department of Justice's 2010 report *School-Based Programs to Reduce Bullying and Victimization*, school-based antibullying programs decreased bullying by **20 to 23 percent.**

- Of participants in Teens on Target, a youth violence prevention program, **75 percent** report that they are very likely to look for alternatives to violent situations after the program, as compared with **31 percent** before.

- The CDC reports that violent crime arrest rates for male youth aged ten to twenty-four years has declined from **850.8 arrests per 100,000** youth in 1995 to **519.6 arrests per 100,000** in 2009, suggesting that prevention efforts are working.

- In a 2010 Gallup poll **68 percent** of respondents would allow the government to prevent sales or rentals of violent games to teens under age eighteen.

# Key People and Advocacy Groups

**American Psychological Association:** The American Psychological Association represents more than 148,000 American psychologists who study and treat human behavior, including youth violence.

**Big Brothers Big Sisters of America (BBBSA):** Big Brothers Big Sisters of America (BBBSA) has been providing adult support and friendship to youth for nearly a century. BBBSA has been designated a model program for youth violence prevention.

**Ronnie Brown:** Brown is an NFL running back who speaks to high school students about youth violence and how to stop it. Brown started "23 WAYS to Stop Youth Violence," an antiviolence campaign designed to raise awareness and give teens practical ways to manage their emotions and behaviors.

**CeaseFire:** CeaseFire is a violence prevention organization that uses its members on the streets to intervene in crises, mediate disputes between individuals, and intercede in group disputes to prevent violent events. CeaseFire staff is composed of seasoned, well-trained professionals from the communities they represent; all have a background on the streets.

**Centers for Disease Control and Prevention (CDC):** The CDC has been studying patterns of violence since the early 1980s. The CDC publishes fact sheets, research, and articles about youth violence and prevention.

**The Children's Safety Network (CSN):** The Children's Safety Network is a national resource center for the prevention of childhood injuries and violence.

**National Gang Center:** The National Gang Center features the latest research about gangs, and its website links to tools, databases, and other resources to assist in developing and implementing effective community-based gang prevention, intervention, and suppression strategies.

**US Office of Juvenile Justice and Delinquency Prevention (OJJDP):** The Office of Juvenile Justice and Delinquency Prevention provides national leadership, coordination, and resources to prevent and respond to juvenile delinquency and victimization.

**STRYVE (Striving to Reduce Youth Violence Everywhere):** STRYVE is a national initiative led by the Centers for Disease Control and Prevention (CDC) to prevent youth violence before it starts among young people aged ten to twenty-four. STRYVE takes a public health approach to youth violence and provides guidance to communities on how to prevent it.

# Chronology

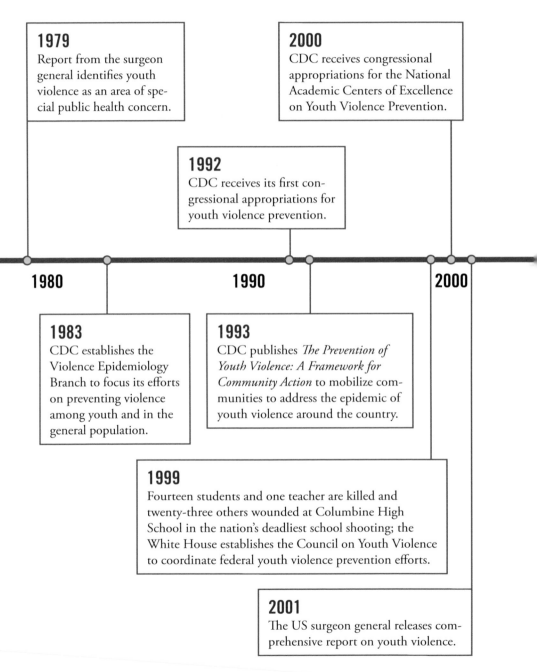

**1979**
Report from the surgeon general identifies youth violence as an area of special public health concern.

**2000**
CDC receives congressional appropriations for the National Academic Centers of Excellence on Youth Violence Prevention.

**1992**
CDC receives its first congressional appropriations for youth violence prevention.

**1980**

**1990**

**2000**

**1983**
CDC establishes the Violence Epidemiology Branch to focus its efforts on preventing violence among youth and in the general population.

**1993**
CDC publishes *The Prevention of Youth Violence: A Framework for Community Action* to mobilize communities to address the epidemic of youth violence around the country.

**1999**
Fourteen students and one teacher are killed and twenty-three others wounded at Columbine High School in the nation's deadliest school shooting; the White House establishes the Council on Youth Violence to coordinate federal youth violence prevention efforts.

**2001**
The US surgeon general releases comprehensive report on youth violence.

**2002**

The World Health Organization releases the *World Report on Violence and Health*, which includes a section focused on youth violence.

**2005**

California passes a law banning the sale to minors of video games with an M, or mature, rating.

**2010**

Study conducted at Texas A&M International University finds no link between violent video games and youth violence.

**2010**

**2004**

The National Youth Violence Prevention Resource Center (NYVPRC) is launched as a clearinghouse of information for people and organizations interested in preventing youth violence.

**2009**

The brutal beating death of Chicago high school honors student Derrion Albert sparks outrage among community and national leaders.

**2011**

The Supreme Court strikes down the 2005 California ban on sales of M-rated games to minors.

**2012**

Gunman T.J. Lane kills three students and injures several others in a shooting at Chardon High School in Ohio.

# Related Organizations

### American Psychological Association (APA)

750 First St. NE
Washington, DC 2002-4242
phone: (800) 374-2721
e-mail: public.affairs@apa.org • website: www.apa.org

The American Psychological Association represents more than 148,000 American psychologists who study and treat human behavior. The association's website features information about psychology topics, including youth violence, and contains links to many publications.

### Centers for Disease Control and Prevention (CDC)

1600 Clifton Rd.
Atlanta, GA 30333
phone: (800) 232-4636
e-mail: cdcinfo@cdc.gov • website: www.cdc.org

For more than sixty years, the CDC has protected health and promoted quality of life through the prevention and control of disease, injury, and disability. The CDC has been studying patterns of violence since the early 1980s. Its website features numerous fact sheets, studies, and information about youth violence, including its causes, prevention efforts, and other related topics.

### Futures Without Violence

100 Montgomery St., The Presidio
San Francisco, CA 94129
phone: (415) 678-5500 • fax: (415) 529-2930
website: www.futureswithoutviolence.org

Futures Without Violence, formerly Family Violence Prevention Fund, works to end violence against women and children around the world. The organization's website provides articles, fact sheets, and information about teen violence and prevention efforts.

Related Organizations

## National Alliance for Safe Schools (NASS)

PO Box 335
Slanesville, WV 25444-0335
phone: (304) 496-8100 • fax: (304) 496-8105
e-mail: nass@frontiernet.net • website: www.safeschools.org

The National Alliance for Safe Schools is a not-for-profit corporation that provides technical assistance, staff training, school safety assessments, safe-school plans, and emergency response training to individual schools and school district personnel. The organization's website features workshops, books, and CDs with information about youth violence.

## National Crime Prevention Council (NCPC)

2001 Jefferson Davis Hwy., Suite 901
Arlington, VA 22202-4801
phone: (202) 466-6272 • fax: (202) 296-1356
website: www.ncpc.org

The National Crime Prevention Council's mission is to be the nation's leader in helping people keep themselves, their families, and their communities safe from crime. The council's website features articles and press releases on a variety of youth violence and violence prevention topics.

## National Criminal Justice Reference Service (NCJRS)

PO Box 6000
Rockville, MD 20849-6000
phone: (800) 851-3420 • fax: (301) 519-5212
website: www.ncjrs.gov

Established in 1972, the National Criminal Justice Reference Service is a federally funded resource offering justice and drug-related information to support research, policy, and program development worldwide. The service's website features articles, statistics, and research on youth violence, gangs, and violence prevention.

## National Gang Center

PO Box 12729
Tallahassee, FL 32317
phone: (850) 385-0600 • fax: (850) 386-5356
e-mail: information@nationalgangcenter.gov
website: www.nationalgangcenter.gov

The National Gang Center website features the latest research about gangs; descriptions of evidence-based, antigang programs; and links to tools, databases, and other resources to assist in developing and implementing effective community-based gang prevention, intervention, and suppression strategies.

## Office of Juvenile Justice and Delinquency Prevention (OJJDP)

810 Seventh St. NW
Washington, DC 20531
phone: (202) 307–5911
website: www.ojjdp.gov

The Office of Juvenile Justice and Delinquency Prevention provides national leadership, coordination, and resources to prevent and respond to juvenile delinquency and victimization. The OJJDP website has the latest juvenile justice statistics as well as fact sheets and articles about youth violence and prevention topics.

## Students Against Violence Everywhere (SAVE)

322 Chapanoke Rd., Suite 110
Raleigh, NC 27603
phone: (866) 343-7283 • fax: (919) 661-7777
e-mail: info@nationalsave.org • website: www.nationalsave.org

SAVE is a student-driven organization. Students learn about alternatives to violence and practice what they learn through school and community service projects. The SAVE website has facts, statistics, and articles about youth violence topics, as well as information about local chapters of the organization.

## US Department of Justice (DOJ)

950 Pennsylvania Ave. NW
Washington, DC 20530-0001
phone: (202) 514-2000
website: www.justice.gov

The Department of Justice enforces the laws of the United States, ensures public safety, and provides federal leadership in preventing and controlling crime. The department website provides statistics about youth violence and crime.

# For Further Research

## Books

Lori Hile, *Gangs.* Chicago, IL: Heinemann/Raintree, 2012.

Henrietta M. Lily, *Dating Violence.* New York: Rosen, 2012.

Jenny MacKay, *Bullying.* Detroit: Lucent, 2013.

Jenny MacKay, *The Columbine School Shootings.* Detroit: Lucent, 2010.

Cindy D. Ness, *Why Girls Fight: Female Youth Violence in the Inner City.* New York: NYU Press, 2010.

Marilyn E. Smith, Matthew Monteverde, and Henrietta M. Lily, *School Violence and Conflict Resolution.* New York: Rosen, 2013.

Richard Swift, *Gangs.* Toronto: Groundwood, 2011.

## Periodicals

Andrew Cauthen, "CDC: Teen Dating Violence 'Serious Problem,'" *Champion Newspaper* (Decatur, GA), June 19, 2012.

*Economist*, "No Killer App; Violence and Addiction," December 10, 2011.

*Florida Times-Union* (Jacksonville), "Video of Chicago Teen Beating Illustrates Internet's Effects in Offline World," January 18, 2012.

Judy Keen, "Teen's Death a Call to Action," *USA Today*, October 8, 2009.

Kim Krisberg, "Ohio Project Working to Educate Teens About Dating Violence," *Nation's Health*, May/June 2011.

Kari Lydersen, "Trying to Survive: Chicago Teen Keeps His Head Up Even After Taking a Bullet to the Chin," *Chicago Reporter*, February 1, 2012.

Kristen Mack and Stephanie Banchero, "Melee Shatters an Oasis for Teens," *Chicago Tribune*, September 26, 2009.

Mary Niederberger, "It's a SNAP: Techniques That Reduce Aggression in Boys Work for Girls, Too," *Pittsburgh Post-Gazette*, July 3, 2012.

Don Petersen, "Post-Columbine Programs Help Prevent Rampages," *USA Today*, April 13, 2009.

Roni Caryn Rabin, "A Cascade of Influences Shaping Violent Teens," *New York Times*, November 18, 2008.

Craig Schneider and Katie Leslie, "Teen Beating Death: They Just Kept Kicking Him," *Atlanta Journal Constitution*, November 8, 2010.

## Internet Sources

American Psychological Association, "Warning Signs of Youth Violence," Just the Facts. http://hr.osu.edu/worklife/youthviolence.pdf.

Centers for Disease Control and Prevention, "Understanding Youth Violence." www.cdc.gov/ViolencePrevention/pdf/YV-FactSheet-a.pdf.

Centers for Disease Control and Prevention, "Youth Violence: Facts at a Glance." www.cdc.gov/ViolencePrevention/pdf/YV-DataSheet-a.pdf.

Find Youth Info, "Preventing Teen Violence." http://findyouthinfo.gov/youth-topics/preventing-youth-violence.

Office of the Surgeon General, "Youth Violence." www.ncbi.nlm.nih.gov/books/NBK44294.

# Source Notes

## Overview

1. Quoted in Craig Schneider and Katie Leslie, "Teen Beating Death: They Just Kept Kicking Him," *Atlanta Journal Constitution*, November 8, 2010. www.ajc.com.
2. Quoted in Lynn Sweet, "Holder, Duncan, Daley Chicago Youth Violence Press Conference," transcript, *Chicago Sun-Times*, October 7, 2009. http://blogs.suntimes.com.
3. Quoted in Emily Sohn, "Is Violence in Sports Inevitable?" Discovery.com, March 7, 2012. http://news.discovery.com.
4. Ofer Zur, *Teen Violence, School Shootings, Cyber-Bullying, Internet Addiction, T.V. and Gaming Violence & Teen Suicide: Facts, Ideas, and Actions*, Zur Institute. http://zurinstitute.com.
5. Kansas Safe Schools Resource Center, "Principles for Identifying the Early Warning Signs of School Violence." www.ksde.org.
6. Quoted in Bonnie Rochman, "Why Spanking Doesn't Work," *Time*, February 6, 2012. http://healthland.time.com.
7. Quoted in Phillip Smith, "Drugs Not Driving Gang Violence, CDC Says," Stop the Drug War.org, January 30, 2012. http://stopthedrugwar.org.
8. Quoted in Beth Azar, "Virtual Violence," American Psychological Association, December 2010. www.apa.org.
9. Quoted in Miranda Leitsinger, "Family: Bullying by 'Wolf Pack' Led to Texas Teen's Suicide," NBCNews.com, April 10, 2012. http://usnews.nbcnews.com.
10. Quoted in Leitsinger, "Family: Bullying by 'Wolf Pack' Led to Texas Teen's Suicide."
11. Quoted in Robert Preidt, "Cyberbullying May Call for New Prevention Tactics," MSN, April 23, 2012. http://healthyliving.msn.com.
12. Quoted in CBS News, "Teen Girl-on-Girl Fighting Goes Online," July 7, 2010. www.cbsnews.com.
13. Quoted in CBS News, "Teen Girl-on-Girl Fighting Goes Online."
14. Quoted in "Video of Chicago Teen Beating Illustrates Internet's Effects in Offline World," Jacksonville.com, *Florida Times-Union*, January 18, 2012. http://jacksonville.com.
15. Quoted in *Huffington Post*, "Diane Latiker of 'Kids Off the Block' Mentors South Side Chicago Kids," April 8, 2011. www.huffingtonpost.com.

## What Is Teen Violence?

16. Quoted in Kristen Mack and Stephanie Banchero, "Melee Shatters an Oasis for Teens," *Chicago Tribune*, September 26, 2009. http://articles.chicagotribune.com.
17. Quoted in Colleen O'Brien, "Late Night Teen Violence Plaguing Downtown Businesses," KXLY.com, June 25, 2012. www.kxly.com.
18. Quoted in Byron Pitts, "Chicago Teen on Living Among Violence: I Don't Expect to Have a Future Here," CBS News, June 12, 2012. www.cbsnews.com.
19. Quoted in Pitts, "Chicago Teen on Living Among Violence."
20. Quoted in Kari Lydersen, "Trying to Survive: Chicago Teen Keeps His Head Up Even After Taking a Bullet to the Chin," *Chicago Reporter*, February 1, 2012. www.chicagoreporter.com.

21. Quoted in CNN, "Ohio Town, Students Grieve After 1 Killed, 4 Hurt in High School Shooting," February 27, 2012. http://articles.cnn.com.

22. Quoted in Sarah Bloomquist, "Police: Philadelphia Student, 14, Assaulted Teacher, 60," ABC, February 13, 2012. http://abclocal.go.com.

23. Quoted in Andrew Cauthen, "CDC: Teen Dating Violence 'Serious Problem,'" *Champion Newspaper* (Decatur, GA), June 19, 2012. www.champion newspaper.com.

24. Quoted in Sadie F. Dingfelder, "Ending an Epidemic," American Psychological Association, March 2010. www.apa.org.

25. Quoted in Dingfelder, "Ending an Epidemic."

26. Quoted in Dingfelder, "Ending an Epidemic."

27. Quoted in Ray Rivera, "Newburgh, Where Gangs and Violence Reign," *New York Times*, May 11, 2010. www .nytimes.com.

28. Quoted in O'Brien, "Late Night Teen Violence Plaguing Downtown Businesses."

29. Quoted in Chapin Hall, "CDC Names Chicago Center for Youth Violence Prevention a National Academic Center of Excellence," press release, January 6, 2011. www.chapinhall.org.

## What Causes Teen Violence?

30. Quoted in Roni Caryn Rabin, "A Cascade of Influences Shaping Violent Teens," *New York Times*, November 18, 2008.

31. Indiana University, "When Children Choose Aggression, IU Researchers Study the Cycle of Violence," IU Newsroom. http://newsinfo.iu.edu.

32. Quoted in Rochman, "Why Spanking Doesn't Work."

33. Quoted in Susie Morris, "Peer Pres-

sure, Media Fuel Youth Violence," ABC News, June 13, 2012. http://abcnews.go.com.

34. Quoted in Dean Reynolds, "In Chicago Hospital, 'Collateral Damage' of Gang War Never Subsides," CBS News, July 9, 2012. www.cbsnews .com.

35. Quoted in Steven Reinberg, "U.S. Murder Toll from Guns Highest in Big Cities: CDC," *U.S. News*, May 12, 2011. http://health.usnews.com.

36. Quoted in UCAN, "Teen Gun Survey 2012," Uhlich Children's Advantage Network. www.ucanchicago.org.

37. Quoted in Casey McNerthney, "For Teens, Illegal Guns Easy to Get on Streets," *Seattle P-I*, September 1, 2008. www.seattlepi.com.

38. Quoted in Lisa Kaiser, "What Are the Causes of Youth Violence?," *Express-Milwaukee*, August 10, 2011. www .expressmilwaukee.com.

## How Do Media Influence Teen Violence?

39. Quoted in Matea Gold, "Kids Watch More than a Day of TV Each Week," *Los Angeles Times*, October 27, 2009. http://articles.latimes.com.

40. Quoted in Gold, "Kids Watch More than a Day of TV Each Week."

41. Quoted in Gold, "Kids Watch More than a Day of TV Each Week,"

42. American Academy of Pediatrics, "Media Violence," October 19, 2009. http://pediatrics.aappublications.org.

43. Quoted in *ScienceDaily*, "Too Many Children See Extreme Violence in Movies," August 4, 2008. www.sci encedaily.com.

44. Quoted in Lloyd de Vries, "Study: TV Violence Begets Violence," CBS News, February 11, 2009. www.cbs news.com.

45. Quoted in *Current Events*, "Should

Kids Play Violent Video Games?,"
September 5, 2011, p. 7.

46. O. Zur, *Teen Violence, School Shootings, Cyber-Bullying, Internet Addiction, T.V. and gaming Violence & Teen Suicide: Facts, Ideas, and Actions*, Zur Institute, 2011. http://zurinstitute.com.

47. Quoted in RadiologyInfo.org, "Violent Video Games Alter Brain Function in Young Men," November 30, 2010. www.radiologyinfo.org.

48. Quoted in *Current Events*, "Should Kids Play Violent Video Games?"

49. Quoted in American Psychological Association, "Playing Highly Competitive Video Games May Lead to Aggressive Behavior," press release, August 29, 2011. www.apa.org.

50. Quoted in Carmela Lomonaco, Tia Kim, and Lori Ottaviano, "Media Violence," Southern California Academic Center of Excellence on Youth Violence Prevention, Spring 2010. http://stopyouthviolence.ucr.edu.

**Can Teen Violence Be Stopped?**

51. Quoted in KSNT.com, "Topeka Police Aim to Prevent Teen Homicide," www.ksnt.com.

52. Quoted in *Pittsburgh Post-Gazette*, "It's a SNAP: Techniques That Reduce Aggression in Boys Work for Girls, Too," July 3, 2012. www.post-gazette.com.

53. Quoted in *Pittsburgh Post-Gazette*, "It's a SNAP."

54. Quoted in Eliott C. McLaughlin, "Interrupting the Cycle of Teen Violence," CNN, September 28, 2011. www.cnn.com.

55. Quoted in McLaughlin, "Interrupting the Cycle of Teen Violence."

56. Quoted in Marilyn Elias, "Post-Columbine Programs Help Prevent Rampages," *USA Today*, April 13, 2009. www.usatoday.com.

57. Quoted in FoxNews.com, "Schools Don't See Teen Dating Violence as a Priority," July 9, 2012. www.foxnews.com.

58. Quoted in Seth Schiesel, "Supreme Court Has Ruled; Now Games Have a Duty," *New York Times*, June 28, 2011. www.nytimes.com.

59. Quoted in Reuters, "Court Strikes Down Minor Violent Video Game Ban," June 27, 2011. www.reuters.com.

60. Quoted in Shirley Henderson, "Stop Killing Our Dreams," *Ebony*, August 2010, p. 80.

# List of Illustrations

# Index

# Picture Credits

Cover: Dreamstime and iStockphoto.com
AP Images: 16
Thinkstock: 12
Steve Zmina: 32–33, 45–47, 59–61, 73–74

# About the Author

Carla Mooney is the author of many books for young adults and children. She lives in Pittsburgh, Pennsylvania, with her husband and three children.